CW01558410

About the author

Dr Charlotte Ritchie is a former researcher at the University of Oxford, and Deputy Director of its Centre for Research into Parenting and Children. She qualified as a social worker in 1997, and was a Senior Lecturer in Social Work at Oxford Brookes University.

CONTENTS

RADICAL CHILD PROTECTION - A PUBLIC HEALTH APPROACH:

Reducing The Number of Children in Care

PREFACE

When the author began training as a social worker it was 1995, the Cleveland inquiry into child sexual abuse was still fresh in everyone's minds, along with children's care home scandals in North Wales, Leicestershire (Frank Beck), Staffordshire (Pindown) and Hackney and the deaths of children such as Dennis O'Neill, Jasmine Beckford, and Maria Colwell at the hands of their parents or foster carers.

A decade later, following the tragic death of Victoria Climbie in 2000, at the hands of her great aunt/guardian and her partner, the Select Committee on Health (Sixth report, 2003) noted that -

> 'The death of any child as the result of non-accidental injury is a tragedy. The fact that in England around 80 children die every year from abuse or neglect, and that this figure has remained relatively constant over more than 30 years, is shocking.'[1]

[1] House of Commons Health Committee Victoria Climbie Inquiry Report 2002-2003 https://publications.parliament.uk/pa/cm200203/cmselect/cmhealth/570/570.pdf

It is now more than 20 years on, and still the number of such child deaths remains relatively constant. Following Victoria Climbie's death and other child deaths, government commissioned reports such as those of Lord Laming (2003, 2009) have led to the tightening up of child protection procedures, and to yet more children being placed in state care. Yet there is no significant correlation between increasing the number of children in care, and child deaths. The numbers remain similar. So what are we doing?

For the past nine years, the number of children in care has steadily increased and at end March 2017, stood at over 72,000.[2] We know the outcomes for children in care, the many thousands filling our prisons, homeless shelters and as adults, our graveyards. Others, with no knowledge of 'good' parenting, go on to parent themselves. It is not all tragedy; many go on to lead fulfilling lives, but we are concerned here with the thousands whose lives are blighted, or at worst, lost.

This book begins by exploring the historical context for current policy and practice, which has so singularly failed our children, and suggests new policy approaches, rooted in public health and our legal framework, and targeted at preventing child deaths, radically reducing the number of children in care, and promoting child and family welfare. To this end, each chapter is discrete and can be read separately from the whole. Each contains key findings as well as questions for discussion and debate. If we are to improve the lives of our children and families, we must start a new debate. This book is just a drop into that ocean.

---

[2] https://www.gov.uk/government/uploads/system/uploads/attachment_data/file/664995/SFR50_2017-Children_looked_after_in_England.pdf

CHAPTER ONE - THE HISTORICAL CONTEXT

On 31st March 2016, 70,440 children were in the care of local authorities in England, an increase from 69,540 in 2015.[3]In 2015, only 14% of looked after children gained five GCSEs A* to C including Mathematics and English, compared with 53% nationally[4]. Of adult prisoners, 23% have been in care, and approximately 40% of prisoners under 21 were in care as children. In addition 25% of young women leaving care are pregnant or already mothers, and almost half become mothers by the age of 24 despite limited experience, if any, of 'good' parenting.[5]

In the 2013/14 financial year approximately £2.5 billion (gross expenditure) was incurred on the principal looked after children's services in England: 55% of which was on foster care services and 36% on children's homes[6]. Yet despite the poor outcomes noted for many of those in care, the still unfolding scandals of physical and sexual abuse in various care establishments and the very high cost of taking children into care, the overarching policy guiding practice has changed little since the Second World War. Various child deaths and inquiries, such as those into Victoria Climbie or Baby P, have led to changes in social work practice, yet the numbers of children killed by carers remains fairly constant, and still children suffer. So how did current policy come into being, and why is it still maintained?

---

[3] Department for Education (2016) *Children looked after in England (Including adoption): year ending 31 March 2016.*London: TSO. https://www.gov.uk/government/uploads/system/uploads/attachment_data/file/556331/SFR41_2016_Text.pdf

[4] Department for Education, Statistical First Release 34/2015.https://www.gov.uk/government/uploads/system/uploads/attachment_data/file/509965/SFR11_2016_SFRText.pdf

[5] http://www.coram.org.uk/sites/default/files/resource_files/Preventing%20unplanned%20pregnancy%20and%20improving%20preparation%20for%20parenthood%20for%20care-experienced%20young%20people.pdf,accessed 15/5/2017
Department for Education,Children looked after in England including adoption: 2009 to 2010. Stastical First Release 27/2010

[6] Department for Education, Statistical First Release 34/2015.

1. SETTING THE SCENE

The nineteenth century was punctuated by a growing interest in the welfare of the young, the origins of which lay, perhaps, not so much in the discovery of neglect or cruelty, as in the changing economic climate that permitted a reduction in the child labour force and the beginning of 'childhood' as a period of economic inactivity, separate from the tasks of parents, and necessitating occupation or education.

The industrial revolution and the expansion of the British economy had made it commonplace for all members of families, other than 'mere infants',[7] to seek employment. But by the latter half of the nineteenth century, a general rise in wages made it easier for families to keep their children out of the labour market until older, and to a lesser extent, led to a reduction in the proportion of married women who found it essential to work. At the same time, the changing manufacturing base and the increasing complexity of social and economic life, led to a requirement for more training, and to legislation that made school attendance compulsory.

> "the transformation of working-class children from
> labourers to pupils was central to the reconstruction of childhood
> at the end of the nineteenth century."[8]

Yet the tensions underlying the child/working unit dichotomy continued into the early years of the twentieth century, until the advent of minimal social security provision. Until then, those who were unemployed, on low wages, or too sick or old to work depended upon their children's wages, and what had

---

[7] Ashworth, W., 1969, *An Economic History of England: 1870-1913*, Methuen, p.192

[8] Hendrick, H., "Child Labour, Medical Capital, and The School Medical Service, c.1890 - 1918, in R. Cooter, ed., *In the Name of the Child: Health and Welfare, 1880-1940*, Routledge

become by now family traditions, died hard, particularly in the textile industry.

To understand the magnitude of the transition from child labourer to child, it is important to consider the plight of many children in the years immediately prior to the beginnings of 'childhood' and 'child welfarism'. In 1867, for example, it was estimated that 77% of the population of Great Britain belonged to the 'manual labour class' which excluded office workers, shop assistants, foremen, and so on.[9] With no social security to fall back on in times of illness, old age or unemployment (which was cyclical throughout the nineteenth century) parents had little option but to send their children to work if they were to avoid the stigma of the workhouse. One church minister

> "related the story of a boy whom he had recently interred who had been found standing asleep with his arms full of wool and had been beaten awake. This day he had worked seventeen hours; he was carried home by his father, was unable to eat his supper, awoke at 4 a.m. the next morning and asked his brothers if they could see the lights of the mill as he was afraid of being late, and then died. (His younger brother, aged nine, had died previously: the father was 'sober and industrious', a Sunday school teacher.)" - [E. P. Thompson, *The Making of the English Working Class*, p.382.][10]

> Engels wrote:
> "When women work in factories, the most important result is the dissolution of family ties."[11] - [F. Engels, pp.160-165]

---

[9] Hobsbawm, E. J., 1969, *Industry and Empire,* Penguin Books

[10] E. P. Thomspon, 1979, *The Making of the English Working Class,* Penguin Books.

[11] Engels, F.,

Women, forced to work to maintain their families and no longer able to rely on an extended family network, frequently returned to work within three weeks of giving birth for fear of losing their employment. As Perkins[12] has stated:

> "Babies and infants were neglected, farmed out to baby-minders who fed them badly and unhygienically or not at all, and quietened them with Godfrey's cordial and other opiates, to their premature destruction."

In 1833, a survey of married spinners in Manchester revealed that of the 3,166 children born to them, only 1,922 had so far survived.

> "This heavy child mortality among the children of workers . . . may be attributed in part to the general environmental health conditions. It may also have been due to the characteristic deformation and narrowing of the pelvic bones in girls who had worked since childhood in the mills, which made for difficult births; the weakness of infants born to mothers who worked until the last week of pregnancy but above all to the lack of proper child care."

Those children who survived the first few years, and who left the Manchester cotton mills were

> "almost universally ill-looking, small, sickly, barefoot and ill-clad. Many appeared to be no older than seven." [E.P.Thompson, *op.cit*.p. 362]

---

[12] Perkin, H., 1969, *The Origins of Modern English Society 1780 - 1880,* Routledge Kegan Paul.

Thus until economic circumstances, and the political change pursuant to it in the late nineteenth century trimming of the laissez-faire ideology, enabled children to be treated as dependants who required care, they often suffered dearly at the hands of their employers. Nor was concern for their welfare driven necessarily by an empathy with the needs of children or by an understanding of their developmental process. Rather, as Thompson points out:

> "the outcry came from 'interested' parties - landowners hostile to the manufacturers, or adult trade unionists wanting limitation of hours for themselves - or from middle-class intellectuals who knew nothing about it".
> - [E. P. Thompson, *The Making of the English Working Class*]

Thus until the closing decades of the Victorian era, the poor physical and mental condition of the children of the poor, often working long hours on the streets or amidst unprotected machinery, was an economic necessity not only largely tolerated - with one or two notable exceptions - by those whose own children were well dressed and tutored at home, but required by the very classes who, as leisure opportunities, wage and living standards increased towards the end of the century, then censured those whose child-rearing, lack of supervision or poverty represented a threat to the new order of education and dependency.

The beginnings of child welfarism reflected the changes in Britain's economic climate.

> 'The 1870s marked a distinct turning-point. Up to that time, whatever happened to incomes, such reliable indices of social

well-being as death rates (and especially infantile death rates) did not fall significantly. Indeed, it is probable that in urban areas they may have risen during parts of the 'golden decades'. After then they began that almost continuous fall which is so characteristic of developed countries."[13]

The transformation of the working child into an object of education and welfare can be said to represent one of the biggest changes to affect society. Indeed, the extension of childhood, or at the very least of dependency, within a family setting has continued to be the hallmark of this century's history.

The demands of 'modern' science and technology necessitated an educated work force, but the assimilation of the British business classes to the social patterns of the gentry and aristocracy served only to create an ever bigger class divide, as the poor were finally excluded from the 'public schools' for whom they had originally been founded. As Hobsbawm (1969) rather wryly noted:

> "In 1869, they [public schools] were more or less set free from all government control and set about elaborating that actively anti-intellectual, anti-scientific, games-dominated tory imperialism which was to remain characteristic of them."[14]

The Education Act 1870, however, provided for the creation of a national system of elementary education for children between the ages of 5 and 13 inclusive, and from 1880 school attendance was nominally compulsory. From 1891 it was free and by the mid 1890s there was, with the exception of a few rapidly expanding areas, a school place for every child. But aspirations for the

---

[13] Hobsbawm, E. J. 1969, Op.Cit. p.159

[14] Hobsbawm, E. J., 1969, *op.cit.*

families and children who had for so long been used, with scant administrative attention to their welfare, to build up the wealth of the nation were limited.

"before the end of the century it had become possible to ensure that very few children grew up in a state of complete savagery, and that almost all of them were . . . at least taught to sit still, a lesson not without benefits for industry and society."[15]

In 1897, fewer than 7% of grammar school children were working class, and

"Knowledge, especially scientific knowledge, therefore took second place in the new British educational system, to the maintenance of a rigid division between the classes."[16]

In 1902, the administrative system was reorganised, and more secondary schools were to be provided. However, as Hobsbawm notes, the effect of the changes was largely to exclude working class children from higher education.[17]

Thus by the beginning of the twentieth century and prior to the first world war, the welfare of children had advanced little. Moreover, the working class child, often still labouring during this early part of the century, had begun its journey to our present concept of child only as a result of political and economic pressure.

---

[15] Perkin, H., 1969, *op.cit.*

[16] Hobsbawm, E. J., 1969, *op.cit.*

[17] Hobsbawm, E J., 1969, *op.cit.* p.169

Perhaps most importantly for our present concept of childcare, the physical condition of recruits for the Boer wars had raised concerns about the health of the nation and by the end of the century concerns were being raised about the quality of British 'stock'. Fears were expressed as to the possibility that unless something was done, the 'British race' would deteriorate.[18] Eugenicists argued that the problem lay with 'degenerate stock' whilst neo-hygienists proposed education, environmental reform, and good nutrition. Meanwhile, despite the Education Act 1870, which won the right to universal primary education, thousands of children were still working, and as late as 1902, a report of the Home Office and the Board of Education estimated that the child labour force was in the region of 300,000.[*] It was, then, not until the first decade of the twentieth century that the medical profession began to take interest in the working child, and to perceive the health of the nation as being intrinsically bound up with a child's education. For the first time, compulsory education provided medical officers of health with an opportunity to study large groups of children in one institution, and they were to vie with teachers and others for control of their destinies.

The children of the poor had at last become the object of professional and institutional concern not perhaps because they were starving, cold, ill-clad and ignorant but rather because the economic and political needs of the country determined that something should be done.

---

[18] British Medical Journal, lead article, 25 July 1903: pp207-8

[*] a more detailed and reliable survey published in 1914, suggested a total for the UK that was 'possibly consideraly over 600,000'.

2.FIRST STEPS: 1850 - 1920

Prior to the 1880s, provision for orphans, the destitute and those with physical or mental disabilities was haphazard. Many of the voluntary societies ensured that only the children of the more genteel gained access to their services. For example, the London Orphan Asylum founded in 1813 required the marriage lines of the parents to be produced, and it was common practice to expect part payment from relatives. For the vast majority of poor, abandoned, destitute, sick and unemployed the local workhouse loomed. Community networks, weakened by the industrial revolution, still offered support for some, and Jean Heywood records the memoir of Kitty Wilkinson, who although poor herself, took in many of the children who had been neglected by parents who were dying from the 1832 cholera epidemic in Liverpool.

The Poor Law Amendment Act 1834 represented an attempt to reduce pauperism by deterrence. Outdoor-relief[19] was withheld from the able-bodied unemployed, who could receive help only by going into the workhouse, 'where life was to be less attractive than the most unpleasant means of earning a living outside.'[20]Commentators in 1852 stated that they had -

> "seen nothing in the prisons and lunatic asylums of Europe to
> equal conditions in the English workhouse where children, lunatics,
> incorrigible, innocent, old, disabled were all mixed together."[21]

---

[19] After the passing of the Elizabethan Poor Law (1601), outdoor relief was the kind of poor relief where assistance was in the form of money, food, clothing or goods, given to alleviate poverty without the requirement that the recipient enter an institution.[1] In contrast, recipients of indoor relief were required to enter a workhouse or poorhouse. https://en.m.wikipedia.org/wiki/Outdoor_relief, accessed 8/11/17

[20] Heywood, J. S.,1965, *Children in Care: The Development of the Service for the Deprived Child,* p.36, Routledge & Kegan Paul.

[21] Webb, S., 1910, *English Poor Law Policy*, p.38

The removal of out-relief, the continuing existence of unemployment, particularly in the towns, and the separation of families by the workhouse test, led to a common detestation not only of the poor law but of the authorities who carried it out. Men, women and children would often rather beg than suffer the stigma and horror of the workhouse.[22] The concern was not with the welfare of the child or family but with deterrence. The poor law authorities had a duty to care for the child who was destitute, orphaned or deserted, or who came with his family into the care of the parish if the parents were too poor to look after him, but nobody had any responsibility for those who were neglected or cruelly treated in their own homes. Nor did the authorities have any duty to discover homeless children and provide for them.

However, the importance of the children's charities that arose towards the end of the nineteenth century was that unlike other philanthropic charitable organisations and movements, they were driven by a desire to 'rescue' children both from their circumstances, and from their immoral and unchristian ways.

> "Rescue work became the province and expression of evangelical influence . . . it became separated from the more analytical charity which developed from the teaching of the organised schools of thought, aimed at preventing the causes of distress . . . So the workers in the field saw their urgent duty not only as an opportunity to rescue children from neglect and cruelty and desertion in all its forms, but also to bring souls to the kingdom of heaven."[23]

---

[22] See, for example, Thompson, E. P., 1968, *The Making of the English Working Class,* Penguin

[23] Heywood, J. S., 1965, *op.cit.* p.50.

15

The distinction is important in so far as the crusading zeal of the early charities, and of individuals such as Dr. Barnardo and Benjamin Waugh quickly created a 'lobby' whose emphasis on 'rescue' or 'protection' was far greater than on prevention. As a result, a vacuum was created at the preventive end of the continuum which could be filled only, as we shall see, by the medical and educational authorities working within a statutory framework.

In 1862, Dr Barnardo became a Christian following a revivalist meeting. He opened a Ragged School in Stepney and soon realised that many children - whom Barnardo thought to be aged 9 to 14 - were living on the streets.

> "it seemed as though the hand of God Himself had suddenly
> pulled aside the curtain which concealed from my view the
> untold miseries of forlorn child-life upon the streets of London."[24]

By 1870 he had opened the first 'Home for Destitute Boys' at No.18 Stepney Causeway, where destitute boys living on the street could stay. Above the doorway he affixed the sign, 'No Destitute Child Ever Refused Admission'. But there seems to have been relatively little understanding of why such children were on the streets. No doubt some had run away from homes where they had been ill-treated, but many may have seen street life as a better alternative to the workhouse, or to the poverty and neglect enforced on children whose parents were unemployed, sick, or too hard at work to be able to 'care'. It is worth remembering, too, that for decades society in general had shown little or no interest in children as the objects of love or care, and no doubt the expectations of parents and children alike were grounded in the reality of their battle for survival outside the workhouse.

---

[24] Cited in Williams, A. E., 1953, *Barnado of Stepney*, pp.60-61, Guild Books.

Thus the 1870 Education Act compelling London children below the age of 13 to attend school regularly, led to the beginnings of protectionism. For many of the street children

> "preferred their wild mature freedom and the shelter of their
> temporary lairs to the thought of compulsory school and
> discipline linked with the shelter of a Home."[25]

Thus Barnardo found that persuasion and constraint were necessary in his work. Yet Barnardo and others like him who seemingly felt sure of their moral superiority compared to the values of the poor, seemed to have had little doubt about the worth of their actions.

> "If the children of the slums can be removed from their surroundings
> early enough, and can be kept sufficiently long under training, heredity
> counts for little, environment counts for everything"[26]

The promise of the early rescuers was that they did not, unlike the supporters of eugenics, consider the poor to be of wholly degenerate stock, but they nonetheless saw little virtue in the bonds of family life. In 1881, the Waifs and Strays Society (now known as the Church of England Children's Society) opened its first home in East Dulwich, and in 1884 Benjamin Waugh, a Congregational minister formed the National Society for the Prevention of Cruelty to Children.

In 1869, Thomas Bowman Stephenson, a Wesleyian minister, also began to open homes for destitute boys -

---

[25] Heywood, J. S., 1965, *op.cit.* p.52

[26] Cited in Williams, A. E., 1953, *op.cit.* p. 95-96

"they *needed*[*] a friend and a home - someone to tell them of
God and to teach them a trade."[27]

Again we see the sure knowledge of the rescuer as to what the children, about whom and about whose way of life, after all, Stephenson really knew so little, needed. The essential point is that the early rescuers provided a template that it has proved impossible to remove. In believing that the children could be given a better life away from their parents, they seemed to ignore the emotional and cultural values of others, and most importantly, their poverty. Whilst it may be true that by taking in some children, they saved their families the fate of the workhouse, there is in their work not a hint of radical policy or reforming zeal. Although individual officers may have had an understanding of the difficulties and hardships faced by the families of the poor, they did not seek to challenge the ideology of the ruling classes that such families were generally indolent, degenerate or just plain bad.

All the rescue societies used emigration fairly extensively, sending children as far afield as Australia, New Zealand, South Africa and Canada, and signifying their belief that emigration ensured that children could not return, as indeed they tended to do, to their 'bad' family surroundings. It is a monument to the moral superiority of the powerful, that the practice continued into the 1950s. In the early years and beyond -

> "Special receiving Homes were set up in the new
> countries to which the children could go and stay for
> a short while to become acclimatised and to get to know
> the agent who would supervise them in their new home.

---

[*] Own italics

[27] Cited in Walpole, C. F., 1947, *The Silver Stream,* p. 39-40, Epworth Press.

It was, however, a difficult and tricky business and, by
the loneliness and isolation, laid the child open to grave
abuse."[28]

There was no statutory supervision of the voluntary agencies, and thus
Barnardos and others - no doubt believing themselves right - exposed
thousands of children to permanent abandonment abroad, and abuse. It is
easy, with the benefit of hindsight, to criticise, and no-one doubts the good
intentions of most of those involved. It is beyond question that Barnardo was
a man of conviction and integrity who was greatly moved by the suffering of
poor children, but these children were arguably not for the most part at risk of
death or even injury; they were poor and behaved in ways that he found
disturbing. In rescuing them, he and others like him, set in train a
protectionist mentality that found its justification in moral superiority. The
reformers themselves were not 'like that', and nor were their children. The
practice of sending the children of the poor far away to outposts of the empire
was not new; vagrant children had been sent to the colonies in the 17th
century, but its promotion and expansion was, and continued into the 1970s
with the children's charities at the fore. As Pat Starkey notes -

'The main pressure for child rescue and the religious impulses which powered
it can be laid at the door of four men, Thomas Barnardo, Thomas Bowman
Stephenson, Edward de Mountjoie Rudolf and Benjamin Waugh, the
founders of Dr Barnardo's Homes, National Children's Homes, the Church of
England Central Homes for Waifs and Strays and the National Society for the
Prevention of Cruelty to Children (NSPCC). Their success in attracting
financial and other support for their work owed much to the skill with which
they tailored their publicity to contemporary ideas about childhood, the
threats posed to the ideal by urban life and the irresponsibility, as they saw it,

[28] Heywood, J. S., 1965, *op.cit.* p.62

of many poor parents. They constructed a picture which permitted the conclusion that removal of children from poor and inadequate homes was a Christian duty and in the best interests of the child.'

It was not until 2010 that the British government offered its apologies and as we shall see, inquiries into historical abuse continue.

The problem for researchers and historians is that all too frequently the voices of the poor and disempowered have been lost. For the most part unable to write, their stories were seldom documented.

Until 1889 rescue societies had no rights of custody. That is not to say that delinquents could roam free. The Infant Felons Act 1840, and the Reformatory Schools Act 1854, provided for the care of young offenders. But the mother who wanted her child back from, say, Barnardos, had to seek a writ of habeas corpus[29]- not easy, for example, for a poor widow, with little confidence and no money for the lawyer. Interestingly, legislation authorising custody of the rescued child in 1891 followed from an argument between Barnardo and the Roman Catholic Crusade of Rescue over a child whom the Catholic society wished to reclaim. Unfortunately for the latter, Barnardo's had given him to a Canadian gentleman who had stipulated that the boy should have no further contact with relatives and that he should be allowed to take him away without disclosing his future address. So much for protection.

The Poor Law Amendment Act 1889 and the Custody of Children Act 1891 are fundamental to the present structure of child protection in that for the first time legislation gave boards of guardians (today's local authorities) and benevolent institutions powers to assume parental rights. The 1891 Act

---

[29] Habeas corpus is a recourse in law through which a person can report an unlawful detention or imprisonment to a court and request that the court order the custodian of the person, to bring the prisoner to court, to determine if the detention is lawful.

allowed the benevolent institutions to act first in removing a child, and forced parents to prove that they had not abandoned, neglected or ill-treated their children, thus setting the pathway for our modern legal framework, in which it is for the parents to prove that they are capable. Thus the poor were further disempowered. A writ of habeas corpus alone - even if the parent could find the where-with-all to pay for one - did not guarantee return of the child. The Act, the first of many, also opened up the possibility of legal argument as to what constituted abandonment, neglect or ill-treatment - an argument that still finds an echo in the minutes of case conferences and court proceedings today.

Nor has provision for children 'in care' changed to any marked extent. Generally, the boards of guardians, like today's local authorities, were responsible for pauper children - arguably 'children in need' under s.17 of the Children Act 1989 - and had to deal with them out of the public purse, whereas the voluntary societies could afford to experiment with new ideas. The voluntary organisations were empowered by law to act in certain ways, but had no duty to do so, whereas the boards of guardians and from 1871 onwards, the Local Government Board, had a duty to administer the poor law. Poor law children could, from 1862 onwards, be sent to voluntary institutions certified by the Poor Law Board in exchange for payment, much as local authorities today can 'buy in' care. From 1870 onwards pauper children were also fostered, or 'boarded out' although only where all family ties with the family were broken, as it was deemed wrong to separate children too far from their families. By contrast, in 2014, the National Audit Office found that 34% of children in residential care and 14% of foster children were living, at a minimum, more than 20 miles from home (NAO (2014) *Children in Care*).

Although a Mr J. Henley,[30] a century ago, reported that the selection of foster mothers was the keystone of the whole edifice, and that boarding out would not be successful unless there was careful selection of foster-mothers (no mention of the characters of fathers), liberal payment, and supervision by paid officials, little was done until the 1960s. Thus boarding out laid young people open to the worst forms of abuse in conditions that were often no better than those they had left. To many of the foster carers they provided a cheap form of labour. Those who opposed boarding out said that its chief merit in the eyes of the representatives of the ratepayers was that it was cheap. An argument that still finds its proponents today.

Thus during the last decades of the Victorian era a pattern was set for the accommodation of children in care. The voluntary organisations also boarded out, as well as providing accommodation in houses, and purpose built villages. But although there can be no doubt as to the sincerity of the attempt to build a better physical environment for the children, scant attention was paid to the possibility that the parent figures might abuse or ill-treat the children. Indeed, when considering the work of the NSPCC and present day child protection workers it is instructive to remember that beatings were acceptable into the latter half of the 20th century; beatings administered not because, perhaps almost understandably, the parent was tired or even drunk, but because it was felt to be right by the rescuing institutions, reinforced by a Victorian male-dominated culture of discipline. Thus Leonard Shaw, a life-long friend of Barnardo, who set up the Manchester and Salford Boys' and Girls' Refuges, could state that he tried to combine firmness and kindness with the children, whilst admitting that one Benjamin Thatcher had been

---

[30] cited in Heywood, J. S., 1965, *op.cit.* p.82

'flogged 12 strokes for his disruption'.[31] Similarly, Alexander Devine, the founder of the Gordon Boys' Home wrote of punishments -

> "One is the flogging of boys under the age of 14 with a birch rod, the strokes not to exceed twelve. I have seen many juveniles punished in this way".[32]

These were, then, considered acceptable forms of punishment in so far as they were administered by a 'better'class, and could be justified in terms of the child's best interests, or even welfare.

Historians frequently point out that separating the children of the poor from their parents was thought necessary in order to avert the contagion of pauperism, but it seems, too, that pauperism and poverty were associated in the minds of the rescuers with vice and immorality in such a way as to make it inconceivable in the eyes of the charitable that children might be open to just as much risk in their new found surroundings. Pressure for inspection of foster homes was slow to build up, partly no doubt reflecting the belief that the poor law authorities and charities were at least trying to save the children from becoming the next generation of paupers; an ethical consideration that seemed to outweigh considerations of risk to the child. As late as 1909 we still find the majority report of the Royal Commission on the poor laws recommending that boarding out should be the subject of Local Government Board inspections,

---

[31] Shaw, L., 1900, 'After Thirty Years. Manchester: Manchester and Salford Boys' and Girls' Refuges, cited in Cockburn, T., 1995, *Child Abuse and Protection: The Manchester Boys' and Girl's Refuges and the NSPCC, 1884 1894*, Occasional Paper No.42, University of Manchester.

[32] Devine, A., 1890, 'Scuttlers and Scuttling: Their Prevention and Cure', Manchester Guardian, cited in Cockburn, T., 1995, *op.cit.* p. 26.

The latter decades of the nineteenth century saw a plethora of legislation enacted aimed at dealing with the worst excesses of prejudice and poverty. The Infant Life Protection Acts1872 and 1897, and the Bastardy Laws Amendment Act 1872, sought to put an end to the practice of baby farming, whose worst excesses had resulted in notorious trials for child murder and ill-treatment, and whose raison d'etre lay in the financial and social perils facing the illegitimate child and her mother in an age where maintenance, until 1872, was virtually impossible to enforce even assuming the father to be employed. Interestingly the Infant Life Protection Act 1897 also proved to be a precursor of place of safety orders, in so far as for the first time local authority inspectors were given powers to enter a house to remove a child to a place of safety.

The Prevention of Cruelty to and Protection of Children Act 1889 and the Poor Law Act 1899 gave boards of guardians authority to assume all the rights and responsibilities of a parent over a child in care until that child reached the age of 18. The Poor Law Act 1899 expanded the grounds for the assumption of such rights from child desertion alone, to include orphans and children whose parents were disabled, in prison or 'unfit' to have the care of them. Heywood (1965)[33] points out that the 1899 Act represented a clear attempt to lay down a definite standard of parental care with the deterrent that failure to reach the standard would allow the state to intervene and assume responsibility for the child until the age of 18.

But a consideration of the early years of today's system would be incomplete without the NSPCC. Societies for the prevention of cruelty to children, often providing shelters or refuges to street children, had sprung up in thirty-one cities and towns by 1889, and many of them had lobbied Parliament for legislation to protect the unguarded child. In May 1889 the London branch

[33] Heywood, J. S., 1965, *op.cit*

amalgamated with some of the other societies to form the NSPCC, and in the late summer of that year the Prevention of Cruelty to and Protection of Children Bill was enacted. Section 1 set out the benchmark for cruelty -

> 'Any person over 16 years of age who, having the custody, control or charge of a child, being a boy under the age of 14 years or being a girl under the age of 16 years, wilfully ill-treats, neglects, abandons or exposes such a child, or causes or procures such a child to be ill-treated, neglected, abandoned, or exposed, in a manner *likely to cause* such child *unnecessary suffering* or injury to its health, shall be guilty of a misdemeanour.'[*]

It formed the starting point for legal and ethical wrangling over what was to constitute 'likely to' or 'unnecessary suffering', or, for that matter 'injury', which still finds remarkably similar echo in the Children Act 1989, where, for example a ground for an interim care order is given as

> "that the child concerned is suffering, or is likely to suffer, significant harm;"   - section 31(2)(a).

Courts were also given the power to take children out of their parents' care, if convicted of neglect and ill-treatment, and to commit them to the charge of a relative or other 'fit person', including industrial schools and charitable organisations, until the age of 14 for boys, or 16 for girls. It was from this Act, and its successor, the Prevention of Cruelty to Children Act 1894 that the NSPCC drew its strength.

---

[*] Own italics,

The importance of the NSPCC lies in the fact that from the 1880s until 1939 it was recognised as the primary organisation in the formulation of child protection policy. Even now, its research, fundraising and protection work command respect among workers in the field, academics and civil servants alike, with strong implications, as we shall see, for concepts of child abuse today.

From its inception, the NSPCC was dominated by the church in the form of its creator, Benjamin Waugh, a congregationalist, and by the elite of the Victorian middle and upper middle classes. The branch aid committees were dominated by the clergy and members of the local judiciary, and those interests continued to hold sway despite the fact that the participation of working men had been written into the constitution as the Victorian era ended. Women were involved in fund-raising and in running some of the early shelters, but space for them at executive level was rationed.
For example, the Stockton and Thornaby branch stated that the executive was to consist of not more than fourteen members, 'four of them to be ladies'.[34]

By 1914, the NSPCC employed 258 inspectors, and dealt with approximately 55,000 cases per annum. From inception the NSPCC had used fundraising and publicity to draw attention to its work and to encourage those with suspicions of cruelty to come forward. Interestingly Ferguson (1992) records that the Middlesbrough committee's first prosecution resulted in a 'neglectful' shipyard labourer and lone parent of four children being sentenced to three months' hard labour. By 1914, the NSPCC had been responsible for the prosecution of 55,292 families.

---

[34] Ferguson, H., 1992, "Cleveland in History: The Abused Child and Child Protection, 1880 - 1914", in Cooter, R (ed), 1992, *In the Name of the Child: Health and Welfare 1880 - 1940,* Routledge.

The position of the NSPCC within the patriarchal society of the dying days of Empire was the source of its authority and power. Not only were local branch committees and the NSPCC's upper echelons dominated by members of the ruling classes, but women were almost totally excluded from the power structure. The all male inspectorate is described by Allen and Morton, (1961), in their authorised history of the NSPCC.

> "A tradition has grown up over the years for men who have
> retired from the Armed Services, particularly the Royal Navy and
> Royal Marines, to form a large proportion of the Inspectorate; their
> knowledge of their fellow men and their power to command being
> valuable qualities for the work. . . . Only married men are considered
> for appointment since experience has shown that an Inspector's success
> largely depends on the sympathetic support given him by his wife." [35]

Given that the families of sailors, in particular, see precious little of their fathers/husbands, it might seem surprising that such men should have been thought to have the experience of children or childcare to qualify them to pronounce on the fitness of others to parent. But, as the official history of the NSPCC points out -

> "The work calls for qualities of individuality and leadership because,
> perhaps more than in any other branch of social service, these men
> . . . have to work alone . . . they develop their own methods and one
> Inspector will approach problems in a very different way from another;
> his devotion, powers of perception and understanding, and the kind of
> support given him by his wife and by his local committee all entering
> into the equation." [36]

---

[35] Allen, A., & Morton, A., 1961, *This is Your Child: The Story of the NSPCC*, Routledge & Kegan Paul.

[36] Allen, A., & Morton, A., 1961, *op.cit.*

The original purpose of the NSPCC demonstrates clearly how the bifurcation between protection and prevention has been made possible. As R. J. & J. Owen (1987) have pointed out in yet another authorised history of the society,

> "What made the NSPCC different from the others was that
> its main purpose was not to take over the care of children.
> Its aim was - and still is - to ensure, where possible, the safety
> of children within their own home or as Benjamin Waugh put
> it ' to remove the evil from the home, not the child.'"[37]

Within the context of Waugh's day, phrases such as 'the evil from the home' would not have seemed as moralistic and judgmental as they do today, and social work practice today would, perhaps, choose 'abuse' - a word just as hard to define, and in our century perhaps just as damming as 'evil'. In positing the concept of 'evil' in the home, however, Waugh was clearly stating that these families were 'other', different in kind, and perhaps in need of salvation.

It was found, however, that neither 'evil' nor abuse could be easily removed from the home, as they were not independent agents, but properties of adults and circumstance. As little or no consideration had been given to working with adults, partly because the poor were seen as incapable of change, it was the children who had to be 'rescued'. If one parent was convicted, the child would often end up in care as lack of social security provision meant almost certain destitution. But even if the parents were not convicted, the Poor Law Act 1899 gave boards of guardians authority to assume the complete rights and responsibilities of a parent over a child until the age of 18 if the parents were deemed 'unfit' to have the care of them, and magistrates could issue a

---

[37] Owen, R. J. & J., 1987, *NSPCC*, Religious and Moral Education Press.

warrant to be executed by a police officer to enter a house and search for the child, to be detained in a place of safety until he could be dealt with by the court. Thus the Poor Laws still find support in today's s.44 of the Children Act 1989, which formalises the arrangement in an Emergency Protection Order.

Thus the assumption of the rights of care can be seen to be embedded still today in the poor law provision of the nineteenth century. Prosecution of a parent for ill-treatment, for example, would almost certainly mean the child falling into the care provision made available by the boards of guardians under the poor laws of the preceding decades, or by the voluntary organisations, such as Barnardo's. Without this pre-existing accommodation and ideology it is possible to imagine a more supportive role being allocated to the parents, but in the climate of pauperism, degeneracy and moral superiority that marked the declining days of Empire, that was not to be. The effect, however, may arguably have been to burden the twenty-first century with a poor law mentality that has defied the advent of the welfare state.

Ferguson[38] notes that like the system today, the NSPCC also operated an 'arm's length' policy of ensuring that its officers were not, for the most part, local men. Thus the 'cruelty man' as he was often known could maintain a distance from the local populace, although not perhaps so much from the local justices, who were frequently also members of the society's branch committee. During its first twenty years or so, shelters were often provided by the NSPCC in our towns and cities.

> "As symbolic as well as utilitarian institutions, the shelters were
> in many respects a cultural embodiment of the desire to restructure
> existing Victorian welfare practices in the name of the abused child

[38] Ferguson, H., 1992, *op.cit.*

and according to new conceptions of child protection."[39]

Although occasionally used by street children or desperate mothers,
Ferguson's analysis of the Cleveland area shows that they were most often
used by NSPCC officers who routinely took suspected abused children to
them, as well as by the police, school board officials and the public. These
were not quietly run establishments in a residential part of the town, but
frequently sported large signs designating their whereabouts and functions.
These 'places of safety' could also provide the NSPCC with the information
that they wanted for prosecution. As the Stockton child protectors pointed
out at the inauguration of their shelter in 1891:

> "A little kind treatment in such a shelter will do much to open
> the minds of these little ones to tell the tale of their sufferings,
> and it is most desirable that the Officer should have access to them
> in preparation of his case for court."[40]

Thus until the turn of the century, and arguably to this day, the main thrust of
the NSPCC was to focus on the child and to punish the parent, and in so doing
deter others. Although ostensibly concern was for the child, and no doubt
officers were greatly moved by what they saw, the desire to deter and punish
was such that the needs of the child or family were not a primary objective.
Ferguson notes that between 1891 and 1903, more than 800 children were
taken into the Stockton shelter, but that 94% were returned to their parents -

> "either immediately, in the case of a court action not being
> pursued, or usually within 3 months, in the case of one or both

---

[39] Ferguson, H., 1992, *op.cit.*

[40] *STAR*, 1891:8, cited in Ferguson, H., 1992, *op.cit.*

parents being imprisoned."[41]

Ferguson argues that as the number who did not return home at all was but a small percentage of the whole, the NSPCC's work was not so much about 'rescue' as about enforcing parental responsibilities in the home. Yet we know from current research that interventions by enforcing agencies often exacerbate already difficult home conditions.* Moreover, removal of a child that is subsequently found to be unwarranted in 94% of cases can hardly be seen as good practice. Yet this again finds echo in modern practice, where the numbers in care or even on child protection registers represent but a small percentage of those initially investigated. That is not to argue that the 94% were problem-free families or, for that matter, that those who do not end up on child protection registers do not have their own difficulties, but rather that in both cases, little or no support was given.[42]

By the turn of the century, the NSPCC was the largest organisation dealing with cruelty to children,[43]and gained influence by its aggressive advertising policy, often leafleting whole areas asking people to report anything suspicious, or displaying photographs or pictures of the worst cases of malnutrition or beating. In 1891 the League of Pity was formed to encourage young people to help those less fortunate. The latter is interesting in so far as it encouraged those with savings to spare, to look down and pity those who did not. Even today, according to the NSPCC annual report for 2015, its public relations and publicity department uses over 22% of the organisation's annual

---

[41] Ferguson, H., 1992, *op.cit.* p. 163

[42] Gibbons, J., Conroy, S., Bell, C., 1995, *Operating the Child Protection System,* HMSO, London

[43] Ferguson, H., 1992, *op.cit*

income and spends over £28.5 million on publicity and fund raising.[44] This 'marketing' of abuse led Wise[45], as long ago as 1991, to comment -

> "They [NSPCC] represent an image of child abuse which has more to do with the financial needs of the organisation in question, than the everyday reality of the majority of child abuse."

In other words, the only moral response available to the viewer of such photographs is to help the NSPCC rather than to help the child or to question the circumstances that have given rise to such abuse.

Thus although the NSPCC did carry out much preventive and supportive work in the home - they did so increasingly as shelters began to close - they gave priority to fundraising and other activities aimed at protecting abused children. Using NSPCC annual reports for Stockton and Thornaby, Ferguson has argued that the number of children permanently removed from their homes remained at fewer than 1% until 1914, but from 1904 onwards officers were formally obliged to remove suspected abused children to workhouses, hospitals and the cottage homes that had come to supersede the shelter. According to the NSPCC *Inspector's Directory* for 1904[46], in an 'emergency case' the 'interests of the child are superior to rules', thus reflecting a change in tempo that arguably remained in force until Cleveland 1987. As Ferguson[47]points out, by 1914 a pattern had emerged whereby children were

See Cleaver, H. & Freeman, P., 1995, *Parental Perspectives In Cases of Suspected Child Abuse*', HMSO, London, and Hoefnagels, C & Baartman, H., 1997, "A Child Abuse Prevention Strategy", *Child Abuse and Neglect*, Vol.21., 6, pp 557 - 573

[44] Messages from Research, Department of Health, 1995, reported that one in seven of those referred will reach the Child Protection Register NSPCC *Annual Report and Accounts* 2014-2015

[45] Wise, S., 1991, *Child Abuse: The NSPCC Version,* Feminist Praxis.

[46] NSPCC *Inspector's Directory*, 1904

[47] Ferguson, H., 1992, *op.cit*, p.164

systematically removed from their homes on the basis of professional collaborations begun before NSPCC workers had consulted with their legal department.

The Children Act 1908 represented a first attempt to consolidate legislation emphasising the social responsibilities of parents. Again, such legislation finds echo in the legislative proposals of more recent years, ie. courts were given wider powers requiring parents to pay fines for their children's offences. More importantly, perhaps, penalties were now imposed for not only wilful cruelty but also negligence such as the overlaying of children or the unguarded fire that leads to an accident. Such legislation was important in that it set a benchmark for the standard of care required from a parent and opened the gateway to the concept of 'risk'.

With the passing of the shelters and the shift towards an increasing professionalisation of NSPCC officers, charged with decision making about 'emergency' cases, the power to protect moved away from local NSPCC branch committees into the hands of the 'professional' practitioners who surrounded the abused child.

> "In emergency cases, the courts now acted merely to rubber stamp
> the disciplinary action already taken to protect children by the
> professionals."[48]

Thus practitioners gained new powers of discretion and autonomy, and although the numbers of those designated 'emergency cases' or the numbers prosecuted may have been but a small part of the NSPCC's overall work, it was the defining characteristic of it, its name (National Society for the Prevention of Cruelty to Children) and its publicity.

---

[48] Ferguson, H., 1992, *op.cit,* p.164

In 1905 a departmental committee was appointed to consider the question of vagrancy, and the NSPCC devised a scheme whereby inspectors who met vagrant families were required to take particulars of the children, their condition and the adults who accompanied them. The families were registered, and their details held at head office.

> "They [Inspectors] notified the district Workhouse Master that the family were on their way to his institution and informed their colleagues in adjacent branches so that the children could be kept under observation during their journey."[49]

It marked the beginning of registration for the purposes of surveillance, with the underlying hypothesis that these children were in some sense, as yet undefined, 'at risk'. The policy extended into more recent times, and makes all too clear the assumptions upon which it was founded. Of the first Aldermaston march against the Bomb, in Easter 1958, Allen & Morton wrote:

> "A considerable number of children, some of whom were very small accompanied the marchers and as the weather was cold and hostile the Inspectors of the Branches were instructed to make sure that the children were being properly looked after."[50]

No clearer example could be given of the invasiveness of the NSPCC's ideology of protection, which until recent times based its concept of risk less, perhaps, on research, and more on the values of middle England.

---

[49] Allen, A. & Morton, A., 1961, *op.cit.* p.40

[50] Allen, A & Morton, A., 1961, *op.cit.* p.48

It should not be forgotten that by the time of the Children Act 1908, a great many families and children were still living in extreme conditions of poverty, and the divide between rich and poor was immense. Biarritz, Cannes, Monte Carlo and Marienbad, steam yachts, private trains and opulent country houses were the hallmarks of Edwardian England for the rich, yet they represented but a tiny proportion of the population. Only 6% of the population left any property worth mentioning when they died, and only 4% left more than £300. But in 1901-1902 just under 4,000 estates paid duty on a capital value of £19 million, and 149 of them were proved for £62.5 million. Below them, was a solid middle and lower class, representing perhaps 30% of the population. But for the working classes, a century of industrialisation had left a legacy that social insurance and the welfare state had not yet ameliorated. When young men were medically examined en masse for the first time in 1917, 10% of them were totally unfit for service, 41.5% had marked disabilities, 22% had partial disabilities and only just over one third were in a satisfactory shape.[51]

It was against this background that the minority report of the Royal Commission into the Working of the Poor Laws could, in 1909, rail against the failure of the poor laws to relieve destitution, and recommend the transfer of its functions to appropriate departments of the local authorities. It was an historic report in that it recognised the need to deal with destitution and poverty before its existence proved critical to the welfare of families. If 'Boards of Guardians' are replaced in our minds by 'local authorities', the following except still rings true today -

> "The failure of the Boards of Guardians . . . to relieve so much
> of the child destitution, is rooted in the very fact that they
> are Destitution Authorities, with a long established tradition

---

[51] Hobsbawm, E. J., 1969, *op.cit.*

of 'relieving' such persons only as voluntarily come forward
and prove themselves 'destitute'. What is required is some social
machinery, of sufficient scope, to bring automatically to light,
irrespective of the parent's application, or even of that of the
children, whatever child destitution exists."

In this, the minority report suggested the Local Education Authority should be utilised, as it already had the administrative and practical machinery necessary to identify 'destitution'. Most notably for those familiar today with the limitations of s.17 of the Children Act 1989, the report continues:

"An Authority dealing with the child, or with the family, merely
at the crisis of destitution having no excuse for intervening before
or after this crisis, can never cope with the conditions here revealed".

Despite the agitation of Mrs Sidney Webb and others, no legislation followed, although both majority and minority reports could be said to sound the death knell of the principles of deterrence and less eligibility towards the less fortunate, and to herald an era in which support, care and treatment were to take precedence.

The reports also highlight the importance that the education authorities had now gained in monitoring child care. By 1900 compulsory schooling had altered public attitudes to child labour, and although large numbers of children carried on working both in and out of school, there could be no comparison with the conditions of child labour of fifty years earlier. Improvements in medical knowledge and in public health combined, in 1907, to establish the School Medical Service. As Hendrick has pointed out -

"One development above all turned children into attractive research subjects, namely, the opportunities offered to inquirers by compulsory mass attendance".[52]

The increasing numbers of Medical Officers of Health and School Medical Officers, who through annual reports provided various information on specific groups of school age workers, allowed them to claim some expertise in this area of child health. At the same time, an interest in child psychology was burgeoning, and in 1907 the Child Study Society was formed in London, supported by most of the leading contemporary psychologists and educationalists. It served as an 'important arena for exchanges between psycho-medical professionals, teachers and parents', although the tension between the medical and other professions was already well established.[53]

Between 1880 and 1900 child labour and health had received little attention in the medical press. The Report of the Inter-departmental Committee on the Employment of School Children (1902) did note that working weeks of 30, 40 or 50 hours for children were detrimental to their health, morals and education, but despite the efforts of George Newman, who later became Chief Medical Officer at the Board of Education, and others to draw attention to the link between poor health and child labour,and the establishment of the School Medical Service from 1907 onwards, the advent of the first world war had still led to an increase in child labour. It was not, therefore, until 1918 that legislation encouraged the medical examination of wage-earning children and imposed a duty on local education authorities to provide medical examinations of adolescents under the age of 18 entering certain institutions.

[52] Hendrick, H., 1992, "Child Labour, Medical Capital, And The School Medical Service c.1890-1914", in Cooter, R. [Ed.], *In The Name of The Child: Health and Welfare 1880-1940*, Routledge.

[53] Hendrick, H., 1992, *op.cit.*p.48

Interestingly, Hendrick notes[54]that in the report of the School Medical Service for 1909, a new chapter had appeared entitled 'Following Up', in which the roles of parents, teachers, attendance officers, nurses and care committee workers were described. By1910, the roles played by the doctor and parent in 'following up' were carefully set out, and by 1911 -

> 'the work of the MO in 'Following up' was treated separately from that of 'the parent', leaving little doubt as to who was the senior partner.'[55]

The SMS also successfully claimed hygiene, mothercraft, education, infant welfare and the co-ordination of the provision of school meals, as part of its portfolio.

From 1910 onwards there were School Medical Officers in each authority, able compulsorily to inspect every schoolchild, and supported by public funds. The Local Authorities (Medical Treatment) Act 1909 allowed the creation of school clinics where children could be treated as well as inspected, so that by 1914, 241 out of 317 local education authorities were giving some form of medical treatment. But it should be remembered that in parallel with this neo hygienist approach, ran the neo eugenicists,[56] who still argued that biological factors explained poor stock, or in today's terminology, multi-problem families. Their work was to be influential until the second world war, where its culmination in the concept of an Aryan race, with all the brutality that ensued discredited it for decades to come.

---

[54] Hendrick, H., 1992, *op.cit.*

[55] Hendrick, H., 1992, *op.cit.*

[56] See Dugdale, R, 1887, 1910, "The Jukes" in Wade, R, (Ed), *The Rise of Urban America. A Record andStudy of Relations of Crime, Pauperism, Disease ;and Heredity,* New York, Arno Press. Also, Davenport, C., 1911, *Medicine and Society in America,* (reprint), New York, Arno Press; Goddard, H., 1914,(reprinted 1972), *Feeble-mindedness: Its Causes and consequences,*Hallandale, FL: New World Book Co., and Androp, S., 1935, *Genetics and Mental Disorders,* New York: Eugenics and Research Association.

Thus, over the years, despite the decline of prestige vis a vis their rivals in medicine - the consultants - the medical officers of health and school medical officers amassed a body of research upon which reformers and others could draw. In so doing, doctors became 'experts' on various facets of childhood and by 1918, had established their authority in child health and welfare. But the significance of the growth in children's medicine and in the education system lies in how it has manipulated our concept of childhood. Of course neither education nor health operated in a vacuum. The need for a more educated populace to meet the technical and scientific advances of the new century had acted as a spur to the provision of universal education at a time when advances in medical knowledge increased the power of the profession. The result of the converging interests of educationists, doctors, and reformers alike was to objectify the child in a way unknown in English history. The working-class child who had but a century before swept chimneys, and who had in their parents' generation worked from a young age in the textile mills or on the streets selling matches or sex was now to be seen as vulnerable, ignorant, immature, irresponsible, dependent and innocent - in fact, a child in need of protection.

3. THE MIDDLE YEARS: 1920 - 1989

The late Victorian and early Edwardian years had witnessed the advent of the child as a dependant, and as an object of medical, educational, and social concern. The years following the Great War, in which men were first able to vent their emotions at the futility of the carnage around them, were to expand the sphere of influence to psychology as well. They were also to confirm women as responsible for every aspect of childhood, bar material support. The dominance of hygienists over eugenicists in Britain, if not in Germany, had also led, by now, to a conviction among many that prevention, environmental change and support were important to welfare.

By 1918, 6.26% of all live births in England and Wales were of babies born illegitimately. The stigma of illegitimacy was to continue into the late 1960s, denoting the strength of a patriarchal society that recognised only children owned by men. In the same year, 1918, the death rate in the first year of life was 186 per 1,000 compared with 91 per 1,000 among babies legitimately born.[57] Many of those born illegitimately thus ended up in care or dead. Legislation such as the Bastardy Law Amendment Act 1872 and the Infant Life Protection Act 1897 (which sought to end the practice of baby farming) had attempted to deal with the worst consequences of society's inability to safeguard the lives of the new born, but the growth of child health and welfare interests following the advent of compulsory schooling opened the way for more supportive agencies, such as, in 1918, the National Council for the Unmarried Mother and Her Child. The Adoption and Legitimacy Acts of 1926 soon followed, enabling the legitimisation of children after marriage, and the legal adoption of children.

---

[57] Heywood, J. S., 1965, *op.cit.*

The loss of so many men in the First World War now made the survival of children and a high birth rate of national importance. Thus Urwin and Sharland[58]argue that

> "From its inception the science of 'mothercraft' was inextricably linked to national priorities of increasing infant survival and maintaining an orderly population capable of adjusting to the demands of industry or the Army."

In 1917, Truby King visited England, and following the opening of the Mothercraft School in Highgate for the training of health visitors, nurses and other professionals, the Mothercraft Manual was published. It was to remain the major source of orthodoxy on infant care and management for the next thirty years. The early editions urged mothers to see child rearing as a matter of national rather than personal concern.

Much of Truby King's work was based on 'scientific' discoveries such as the importance of fresh air, vitamins and bowel regularity. It was held that if the child was brought up this way, he would - all things being equal - become a healthy and sound child. Other professionals were trained in his teachings and based their judgments of good mothering (fathers were not generally held responsible, other than by Freud) upon his work, and that of others who were to follow. Those therefore who chose to bring up their children differently, were to be treated with suspicion, for 'poor mothering' was seen as a precursor to deviance. Lack of regularity in babyhood, for example, was held responsible not only for hysteria, epilepsy and imbecility, but also for other

---

[58] Urwin, C & Sharland, E., 1992, "From Bodies to Minds in Childcare Literature: Advice to Parents in Inter-War Britain', in Cooter, R., (Ed), *op.cit.* p.174

41

forms of degeneracy or conduct disorder in adults.[59]Such thinking now provided the rationale for intervening in the process of parenting.

In 1928, John Watson, an American behaviourist, had published his influential 'Psychological Care of Infant and Child' in which love was seen as a matter of conditioning, which was to be avoided in excess. Again, science was proof that this was so.

> "It is a serious question in my mind whether there should
> be individual homes for children - or even whether children should
> know their own parents. There are undoubtedly much more scientific
> ways of bringing up children which will probably mean finer and
> happier children."[60]

Even Marie Stopes, who produced the infant care manual 'Radiant Motherhood' stressed the importance of routines and regimes, and insisted on scientific rationality as central to liberating women from the bondage of maternity.

The1920s can be seen as a period in which the national need for a new stock of healthy, sound children vied to some extent with the new psychology, whose roots were strengthened by the introspection born of the horror and shock of the Great War, in which officers - men not of 'poor stock' - had been known to break down. It was now possible that the will and the emotions were not driving behaviour which could be controlled by conditioning, but were part of an individual psychology. Moreover, the depression of the late 1920s and early 1930s made it specious to argue that the unemployed were feckless, of bad character or degenerate stock. The growing belief that children and

[59] King, T., 1925, *Feeding and Care of Baby*, Macmillan, London.

[60] Watson, J. B., 1928, *Psychological Care of the Infant and Child*, Allen & Unwin, London. pp 5-6

adults could be 'treated' led to a sharp drop, for example, in the number of boys committed to reformatories and industrial schools. The focus now turned towards early intervention and prevention.

Similarly following the establishment of the Child Guidance Council in 1927, the 1920s and 1930s brought an expansion in the number of child guidance clinics to which doctors and other professionals could refer, and to which parents could also self refer. It marked acceptance of the possibility that change could be made within the family, and that 'disorders' were not fixed, but it also opened the door to delineating a range of childhood disorders that were to come, more and more, within the province of psychiatry. In the wider context, as Urwin and Sharland point out,[61] behaviourism and the enforcement of rigid habits became identified with 'Prussianism' and lost ground to the new psychology and psychiatry that stressed the importance of the child within the family.

The Children and Young Persons Act 1933, although a consolidating measure, can also be seen to reflect an apparent change away from blame and retribution and towards welfare. The Court must now 'have regard to the welfare of the child'. However, contrary to the assumption within the Children Act 1989 that the 'welfare of the child' is in some way a known entity upon which individual judges are able to pronounce, the 1933 Act, as Heywood points out,[62] expressly allayed doubts about the propriety of sending a child of good character away for years, by praying in aid the welfare of the child couched in terms of education and training. Section 44 states:

> "Every court in dealing with a child or young person who is
> brought before it, either as being in need of care or protection

---

[61] Urwin, C. & Sharland, E., 1992, *op.cit.*

[62] Heywood, J. S., 1965, *op.cit.*

or as an offender or otherwise, shall have regard to the welfare
of the child or young person and shall in a proper case take steps
for removing him from undesirable surroundings, and for securing that
proper provision is made for his education and training."

But the 1933 Act also contains within it the lack of definition that remains the
hallmark of modern legislation for children, and which gives strength to the
prevailing ideologies of health and welfare. Thus section 61 states that

"A child or young person, who having no parent or guardian or a
parent or guardian *unfit* to exercise *care* and guardianship, is
either falling into *bad associations*, or exposed to *moral danger*
or beyond control or is *ill treated or neglected* in a manner
likely to cause his unnecessary *suffering* or injury to *health*".

can now be defined as in need of care or protection.

The italics are my own, indicating the alarming lack of definition that served
not only to strengthen the arm of those seeking to take a child into care, but
also ultimately to underpin the rationale for their actions. As we shall see, the
situation is little changed today. Notably, the Act also gave local education
authorities the primary responsibility for bringing children in need of care or
protection to court.

Once again, war was to prove a watershed in academic and popular feeling
about the child and family. The austerity of the 1920s and 1930s had
continued the trend towards smaller families, but the advent of the second
world war placed an added value on family life. In December 1939, a letter in
the British Medical Journal, signed by the paediatrician and psychoanalyst
Donald Winnicott, the child psychiatrist Emanuel Miller and the child

psychiatrist and psychoanalyst John Bowlby warned against the dangers of evacuation. It referred to Bowlby's research at the London Child Guidance Clinic which showed an apparent causal connection between early separation from parents and later delinquency.[63] Bowlby's work was to inform decades of thinking, but its importance at the outbreak of war was that it emphasised the importance of the family at a time when the family gained in importance as a bulwark of democracy against the totalitarian power of the state in Europe. Moreover, it continued the trend towards affirming the mother's role in rearing the young.

Interestingly, Heywood[64] notes that the Government's policy of evacuating young children to the country was frequently resisted. Families -

> " refused to remain divided and gradually, in ones and
> threes and then in groups and crowds, they returned to their
> homes and family circle, preferring to stay together under
> danger than to be separated and safe."

Despite the Government's clear attempt to identify risk and to protect children, families seemingly felt that the quality of their lives together was of more value. The sheer volume of numbers, together with the knowledge that life in any event might be short, seems to have prevented prosecutions or court proceedings. For here were families clearly putting their children at risk not of bruising, neglect or abuse but of nightly terror as they sat in damp, dark air-raid shelters that shook with each blast, and of serious injury or death. Yet the suspicion is that the state did not know best, and that even knowing, as we do now, the terrible damage inflicted on London, Coventry, Liverpool,

[63] Letter to the Editor, *British Medical Journal,* 16 December 1939.

[64] Heywood, J. S., 1965, *op.cit.*p.134

Bristol and so on, we too might have acted in the same way. How can we explain this paradox?

It might be argued that the parents' intention was not to cause suffering, and that there was no intention to harm, yet the same might be said of a parent guilty of neglect. It seems, perhaps, possible that people from *all* walks of life, for once facing the same dilemma together, found themselves unable to give the concept of risk precedence over the strength and bonds of family life. Dying together, perhaps, was better than a life without children, and the 'risk' posed by death or injury was maybe not so great to them as a different type of 'risk' posed to *all* the family by evacuation. Perhaps this was a form of 'abuse' that was classless; not something perpetrated by others but by 'us', the middle classes, as well, and as such it was not, and is still not recognised. Put another way, what makes a 'risk' unacceptable may not be its greatness but its type, and its agent.

Winnicott's series of wartime broadcasts to mothers at home with small children served to stress the mother's responsibility not only for physical health, but for emotional and psychological well being as well. By the end of the war, during which many men were away on active service, the myth of the mother as the sole provider of health and well being, with only discipline and wage-earning being left to the father, had been established.

But evacuation had also brought to light the appalling circumstances in which many of the children lived in their family homes. Even in 1961, the authors of an authorised history of the NSPCC could write of evacuees -

> "vast numbers of these families were widely scattered
> throughout the community and their filthy habits, their

maladjustments, their irresponsibility, and their neglect of
their children came as the greatest of shocks to those who
saw these evil things for the first time."[65]

The quotation perhaps illustrates how the subjective value judgments of one sector of society could label and condemn the values and lifestyles of others. Moreover, it should be remembered that the NSPCC was still the main prosecuting authority, and indeed, its prosecution rate increased during the war. Despite the difficulties of trying to keep body and soul together, with husbands away, rationing, and no social security to rely on, the same authors wrote -

"neglect of children by unworthy mothers became more serious
and there was a sharp rise in the number of prosecutions which the
society had to undertake."[66]

Yet despite the apparent views of the NSPCC, concern grew that too much attention had been paid to changing the environment, and too little to understanding the difficulties and needs of 'failing' parents. Moreover, following the death of Dennis O'Neill in January 1945, as a result of neglect and cruelty by his foster parents, concern grew as to the outcomes for those whose environments had been changed. The inquiry under Sir Walter Monckton showed, as such inquiries into care still do today, that there was a lack of trained and skilled workers, and a lack of administrative co-ordination of care. The ensuing Curtis report on the Care of Children sadly bears

[65] Allen, A & Morton, A., 1961, *op.cit.* p.51

[66] Allen, A & Morton, A., *op.cit.* p. 54.

comparison with the Utting report.(1997)[67] and the 2015 Ofsted Report into Children's Social Care.* The Curtis report found that children received a poor quality of care, with a paucity of understanding or affection, and a deplorable shortage of qualified or trained staff.

Corporal punishment was then an acceptable form of discipline, but it is hard to understand some of the apparent complacency in the Curtis report. For example, the report describes as 'curious' a system of punishment found in one residential school[68] whereby -

> "these girls were said to have been locked in their rooms for
> twenty-four hours and to have had restricted diet. This has been
> discontinued. Now the practice is to cut short the hair of the girl
> who absconds. If she absconds a second time, she is given an Eaton
> crop, and twill smock."

Curtis reports that the girl had found this system better than the -

> "Remand Home, where she said that she had been locked in her
> room, had slept in a wooden bed without a mattress and been fed
> on bread and water after absconding from a hospital at which
> she had been receiving treatment."

Although he notes that a subsequent Home Office inspector disapproved of such punishment, the report does not condemn it even though the shaving of a girl's head was known to be a form of humiliation, as had been witnessed

[67] Utting, Sir W. B., 1997, *People Like Us: A Report of the Review of the Safeguards for Children Living Away from Home,* London, HMSO
* Ofsted (2016) *Children's Social Care in England 2015.* https://www.gov.uk/government/statistics/childrens-social-care-in-england-2015

[68] *The Report of the Care of Children Committee,* Cmnd. 6922, 1946, HMSO, London, p.99

only recently, at the end of World War II, when the heads of French women who had 'fraternised' with German soldiers were shaved. Thus the conditions faced by those in care could in some instances be seen as grounds in themselves for protection.

The Curtis Committee also found the after-care of boys and girls leaving the Homes to be a matter of deep concern. Thus recommendation 55 stated:

> "This [after care] should be a matter of deep concern. Great care should be taken to make the children aware of the possible careers open to them. Full use should be made of the Juvenile Employment Service. Girls and boys remaining in Homes on domestic work or work earning money for the Home, should be treated as employees.
>
> Any deprived child going into employment in a strange place should be enabled to get into touch with the Children's Officer of that area. Hostels for boys and girls from the Homes who go out to work should be provided by local authorities where no suitable lodgings are available."

More than sixty years later the same criticisms could be made. The same children are homeless on the streets, unemployed, unable to form relationships; and the same provision for after care is still widely acknowledge to be inadequate.

The ensuing Children Act 1948 gave responsibility for deprived children to one Department, the Home Office, provided for the appointment of local authority children's officers, and attempted to ameliorate conditions for the child in care by reducing the size of homes, etc. The Poor Law finally came to an end, as the powers of local authorities to receive into care children whose parents were unfit or unable to look after them, were increased. As the new Children's Departments were created in 1948, there were just over 48,000 children in care. By 1953, despite the new emphasis on the family, the numbers in care had risen to 65,309, partly due to the increased leaving age of 18 and partly due to a shift away from the use of 'approved schools', towards care under a 'fit person order'.

The final abolition of the poor laws was complemented by the foundation of the welfare state. It represented, as Beveridge saw it, an opportunity to tackle the 'five giants' of want, disease, squalor, ignorance and idleness, and at last offered the poor some relief from the grind of unemployment, poverty, illness and old age. Family allowances, a health service free at the point of delivery, and a policy of redistribution through taxation strengthened not only the individual, as Heywood points out, but the family.[69]

By 1951, when Bowlby published his highly influential monograph on mental health in children,[70] the family was entering a new period. Apparently freed from the physical and mental stresses of deprivation through the advent of the welfare state, its well-being now came to lie more and more in the hands of mother. The growing cost of care provision due to the huge increase in numbers led to the need for the sixth report of the Select Committee on Estimates[71] to state, in 1952:

> "Much frustration and suffering might be avoided if more attention
> were directed towards the means whereby situations that end in
> domestic upheaval and disaster might be dealt with and remedied

---

[69] Heywood, J. S., 1965, *Op.cit.*

[70] Bowlby, J. 1951,*Maternal Care and Mental Health,* A report prepared on behalf of the World Health Organisation as a contribution to the UN programme for the welfare of homeless children.

[71] Select Committee on Estimates, Sixth Report (Child Care), 1951-1952, para.6.7

before the actual break-up of the home occurs."

Thus from 1950 onwards, with the publication of a Government circular[72], more emphasis was placed on prevention, and in some local authorities case workers were appointed to work with 'problem families'. The circular urged local authorities -

> "to arrange for significant cases of child neglect, and all cases
> of ill treatment . . . to be reported to the designated officer, who
> would arrange for such cases to be brought before the meeting
> so that, after considering the needs of the family as a whole,
> agreement might be reached as to how the local services could
> best be applied to meet those needs."

On the protective side, the Children and Young Persons (Amendment) Act 1952 gave local authorities a duty to inquire into the case of any child or young person about whom they received information suggesting a need for care or protection, regardless whether that neglect was intentional.

In the voluntary sector, although the NSPCC had retained its preference for Inspectors to be drawn from the armed services, it had appointed women visitors in 1948.

> "A Woman Visitor doesn't open a new case, nor does she prosecute
> in the way an Inspector can. She works in close liaison with one
> or more than one, Inspector, and he hands over the cases he feels will
> be best helped by her type of supervision and help."[73]

---

[72] Ministry of Health, circular 78/50, dated 31.7.50, and Ministry of Education circular 225/50.

[73] Allen, A & Morton, A., 1961, *op.cit.*

In some ways this may mark the splitting of prevention and protection into two separate options. Moreover, protection was clearly seen by the NSPCC to be the more important task, with the senior employee - male - deciding from his knowledge of child-rearing just which cases required prosecution or protection, and which could be left to a woman. As late as 1962, only 37 women were employed in the field by the NSPCC.[74]

By contrast, a more enlightened view had been taken by the Curtis committee, which had suggested that women might be more suitable for the task of Children's Officer. The children's officer was to be an -

> "excecutive officer with the standing of an important
> administrative official of the council . . . an officer
> of high standing and qualifications".

Men were not to be excluded, but

> "we use the feminine pronoun not with any aim of excluding
> men from these posts but because we think it may be found
> that the majority of persons suitable for the work are women.
> . . . The committal of the child to the care of a council which takes
> over parental rights and duties is not without incongruity. To be
> properly exercised the responsibility must be delegated to an
> individual, and that individual one whose training has fitted her
> for child care and whose whole attention is given to it."[75]

Thus throughout the ensuing period, the prosecution of parents and 'protection' of children remained largely within a male dominated

---

[74] Packman, J., 1968, *Childcare Needs and Numbers,* Allen & Unwin, London.

[75] *The Report of the Care of Children Committee,* Cmnd. 6922, *op.cit.* paras. 441 & 443.

organisation, whose League of Pity - so attractive to the children of the middle classes, with its blue, egg-shaped collecting boxes - looked down upon the poor and their lifestyles, whilst within local government more attention was beginning to be paid to the needs of those who came into its care.

Slowly the preventive arm of social work was growing. The influence of Bowlby and Winnicott was seminal, and combining with the dicta of Keinian psychoanalysis gave birth to a new era in which the mother was denoted as the primary source of emotional stability, whilst the needs of infancy were paramount. Thus there was now a need to see a 'satisfactory relationship' between child and mother, and Urwin and Sharland[76]note that in subsequent childcare literature, becoming an adequate mother took precedence over the problems of managing difficult children.

The continual refocussing of the lens onto the mother is vital to any understanding of child protection today. For although the majority of sexual and physical abuse is perpetrated by men,[77]it is the mother who is frequently the object of assessment, with care in prospect where the mother is thought to be weak in relation not to the children but to the abusing partner. Given that prosecution of abusers is known to occur in only a minority of cases[78]due in part to the difficulties of effecting a successful prosecution,[79] and in part to the difficulties of disclosure, the removal of the child into care can become the only option. This remains the case, not least because the focus remains on the

[76] Urwin, C. & Sharland, E., 1992, *op.cit.* p.194

[77] P & Kempe, C., 1981, *Sexually Abused Children And Their Families,* Pergamon Press, New York. Radford et al (2013) *Child Abuse and Neglect in the UK today,* NSPCC

[78] See Prior, V., Lynch, M & Glaser, D, 1994, *,Messages from Children: Children's Evaluations of the Professional Responses to Child Sexual Abuse,* NCH Action for Children, London.

[79] See Davis, G et al (1999) *The admissibility and sufficiency of evidence in child abuse prosecutions.* London: Research, Development and Statistics Directorate.
Ministry of Justice (2011) *Conviction tables: criminal justice quarterly update for December 2010:* Ministry of Justice Statists Bulletin.
Ritchie, C., *Child Sexual Abuse and the Criminal Justice System,* 1997, MSc thesis, University of Oxford, England.

child, with the abusing parent neither prosecuted/removed or supported - as appropriate.

Confidence in the expanding local authority service was reflected in the Children Act 1958, which for the first time allowed children, under certain circumstances, to be freed for adoption without the parents' consent. At the same time, preventive work was reinforced by the report of the Ingleby Committee, which saw removal of children from the home as potentially destructive, and sought to promote machinery for its prevention via the more efficient detection of families 'at risk'. Thus the assessment of 'risk' became important not only to families, but to the social workers and local authorities whose 'failings' could be laid wide open by a public inquiry.

The ensuing Children and Young Persons Act 1963 further marked a move towards positive and skilled family centred work. Casework in the home was seen as the priority, with removal into 'care' a last resort. Section 1(1) stated:

> "It shall be the duty of every local authority to make available
> such advice, guidance and assistance as may promote the welfare
> of children by diminishing the need to receive children into or keep
> them in care".

Interestingly, section 1 also imposed a duty on local authorities to offer all kinds of help to families in order to prevent the removal of children from home, including 'assistance in kind, or, in exceptional circumstances, in cash'. The pressures formed by public inquiries, economic recession, and the targeting of resources had, by the time of the Children Act 1989, increased the arm of protection and 'risk', and reduced that section 1 'duty' - which is statutory - to a 'power' which is not similarly enforceable. The difference is stark and critical. It means that local authorities do not have to relieve 'need'.

Both the Curtis and Ingleby reports had noted an apparent connection between unhappy childhood and delinquency, and so again, the Act also tried to improve conditions in care. But the early 1960s also saw contrary trends arising. Just as the outcomes for those in care were being challenged with a corresponding increase in preventive work, so in 1962, the publication by Kempe[80]of 'The Battered Child Syndrome' raised once more the spectre of risk. Caffey's[81] work in 1946 had pointed out the injuries suffered by children, but the publicity surrounding Kempe's work was to have more effect. Kempe's emphasis on the finding that children were being battered by seemingly normal, respectable families was to have a huge impact not only on ensuing theories of inter-generational transmission, but also on the assessment of 'risk' and the intervening power of the medical profession. Both parent and child were now to be the subject of investigation by paediatricians and psychiatrists. Doctors in outpatients' departments were to look for signs of bruising or ill-treatment that would identify risk. Cruelty, now abuse, had seemingly been rediscovered with new force, and the following decades were to see the gradual erosion of preventive strategies until the predominance of protection was given formal expression in the Children Act 1989.

Thus by 1966, the number of children in care had risen again, accounting for 5.1 children per 1,000. Moreover the huge variations in the numbers of children committed to care in different local authority areas, still apparent today, led to questioning as to how need could vary so widely. Having established that a 'need' for care was incapable of definition, Packman looked at the reasons given for care applications in fifty local authorities over a six

[80] Kempe, C., Silverman, F., Steele, B., Droegemueller, W. & Silver, H., 1962, '*The Battered Child Syndrome*', Journal of the American Mewdical Association, 181, 17-24.

[81] Caffey, J., 1946, *Multiple Fractures in the Long Bones of Infants Suffering From Chronic Subdural Haematoma,* American Journal of Roentgenology Radium Therapy and Nuclear Mdicine, 56, 163-173.

month period in 1962[82]. She found that for those in long-term care (short-term care being associated largely with parental illness/confinement), the main reasons were illegitimacy, mental illness, homelessness and marital breakdown or death - all factors strongly related to poverty, stress and 'moral'* order. The percentage of care applications under headings that suggest the equivalent of 'abuse' is substantially lower than that given for 1998[83], lending credence to the hypothesis that the rediscovery of abuse from the mid 1960s onwards was to increase numbers in care.

Having considered all the factors that might account for the huge regional variations in the number of those in care, Packman states:

> "One conclusion that can be drawn from this is that children's
> departments can choose whether they admit to care or not and
> do so on the basis of different policies in different places. . . This
> choice might depend upon the availability of other complementary or
> alternative services, the effects of 'rationing' in situations where
> resources cannot meet demand or it might spring from varying
> interpretations of what constitutes need and what does not."[84]

The situation is little different today. As Gibbons, Conroy and Bell[85] noted -

> "Because they [local authorities] operate to different policies

---

[82] Packman, J., 1968, *Child Care Needs and Numbers,* Allen & Unwin, London.

* In 1966, the number of non-offending girls in approved schools was greater than the number of offenders, although most approved school boys were offenders. The factors precipitating admission were 'immorality and promiscuity'.

[83] Department of Health, 1998, *Children Looked After By Local Authorities: Year Ending 31 March 1997 England,* HMSO, London.

[84] Packman, J., 1968, *op.cit.* p.71

[85] Gibbons, J., Conroy, S. Bell, C., 1995, *Operating the Child Protection System,* London, HMSO

and use different criteria it is difficult to compare statistics of children on registers in different areas. Because of this unreliability, national register statistics should not be treated as accurate indicators of the 'true' incidence and prevalence of children in need of protection in different communities . . . the families referred on suspicion of abuse or neglect in one authority were not the same as those referred in another."

Once again, protection seems to depend not so much on concepts of 'risk', 'need', 'abuse', 'proper', 'deprivation' and perhaps most importantly, but arguably least addressed, 'welfare', that defy definition, but on levels of deprivation, available resources and on local historical patterns of care, including poor law provision.[86] Thus, for example, the figures for admissions to care for homelessness, which are not insubstantial, have at their root section 1 of the Children Act 1948, which laid a duty on administrators to decide which children, having parents, should nevertheless be deprived of a home life because they were not provided with 'proper accommodation, maintenance and upbringing.'

Arguably, the attention given to protection also determines the effectiveness of prevention. The Curtis report had stated -

"the Children's Officer would be so well known in her area as the authority on children's welfare questions that individual difficulties and problems would be brought to her as a matter of course."[87]

---

[86] Packman, J., 1968, *op.cit.*

[87] *Report of the Care of Children Committee, op.cit.*para.444

And Ingleby had suggested that -

> "to facilitate the discovery of all families in need of help there
> should be some centre or body to which parents and others know
> they can turn for advice and assistance - some door on which they
> can knock."[88]

But the reformulation of child abuse/cruelty following the publication of
Kempe's paper was to lead to an emphasis on discovery, and, in time, to a
concept of inter-agency working that led not to the open door of support but
to the secretive world of protection.

The work of the NSPCC, particularly in its first thirty years, and the everyday
reality of parents under stress, suggest that Kempe had discovered little new,
that many parents, at least, were not aware of. But what became new, as
Parton has argued,[89] was the 'disease model' of child abuse that dominated
protection at least until the 1980s, when inquiries into Cleveland, the Orkneys
and Rochdale sewed the seeds of doubt as to the number of false positives
thrown up by medico-scientific assessments of abuse or risk, and the validity
of removing children from their homes using emergency powers.

Nevertheless, the welfarism established after the second world war, which
had its roots in joining the fiscal and bureaucratic capacities of the state in
order to motivate national growth and well-being through the encouragement
of social responsibility, still managed to persist. The Seebohm Report 1968
still assumed that social problems could be solved by professionals versed in
social science and relationship skills, employed by the state, and that they

---

[88] *Report of the Committee on Children and Young Persons, op.cit.,* para.14.

[89] Parton, N., 1996, "Social Work, Risk and 'The Blaming System'" in Parton, N (Ed.), 1996, *Social Theory, Social Change and Social Work,* Routledge.

would command community support. Thus the Local Authority Social Services Act 1970 was passed setting up local authority social services departments, whose social workers were thought able, along with the medical profession, to prevent and cure child abuse. The cause of abuse was seen as the parents, and the symptoms could be found in their relationship to the child.

Research centred on the traits of abusing families, and social workers were expected to be aware of these 'known characteristics of child abuse' and to act accordingly.[90]Following the inquiry into the tragic death of Maria Colwell, a Department of Health and Social Security circular (DHSS 1974) stressed the importance of teamwork, and recommended the setting up of case conferences, area review committees and registers. As Otway notes,[91]the medico/scientific model held the commanding role. The problem of the battered child had, by 1974, become 'non-accidental injury to children'.

Thus the 1970s were marked by an increasing awareness of risk, and assessment of actual or predicted risk was seen as increasingly important. But the lack of scientific reliability in risk assessments was to lead to an increasing need for a legal framework, in which the judiciary rather than the social worker could arbitrate on risk through the medium of actual or likely 'significant harm', as set out in the Children Act 1989.

By the end of the 1970s the Labour government had applied to the International Monetary Fund for support, and the economy faced inflation and recession. The advent of the Thatcher government in 1978 brought with it the rise of a neo-liberalism that unleashed market forces upon the public sector, and brought to an end the welfare concept of man as a social citizen,

[90] See Otway, O., 1996, "Social Work with Children and Families", in Parton, N., 1996, *op.cit.*

[91] Otway, O., 1996, *op.cit.* p.155

replacing it with the individual who should earn that citizenship. His rights were to be dependent upon his responsibilities. The Good Samaritan depicted by Mrs Thatcher no longer helped those in need automatically, but was to investigate and assess the situation first.

Resource rationing, as the public sector shrank, served to combine with a targeting of resources on those most in need, or in the case of child care, on those most 'at risk', at a time when new citizens' charters promulgated by a government determined on market forces and 'value for money' led to increased emphasis on professional accountability. The insecurity engendered by the Beckford (1985), Henry (1987), and Kimberley Carlile (1987) inquiries thus led to ever increasing demands for the identification of 'risk' and 'high risk' and to the use of child protection registers, area child protection committees, and child protection investigation teams as tools with which, arguably, to protect children and social workers alike.

The impact was huge. The words of Curtis and Ingleby, and of even more recent reports[92]regarding the poor outcomes for those in care and the need for prevention were lost in the glare of publicity surrounding inquiry after inquiry. The problem now was not that children were dying at the hands of their parents - that had clearly been going on for years - but that the model of risk and abuse offered by Kempe, and the Maria Colwell inquiry[93], and promoted by the resource rationing and targeting of the Thatcher years, still seemed to be failing. Now that the primary function of social workers was seen as protection, failure to protect led to blame, and, in turn with each subsequent inquiry, not to a re-assessment of how the system engaged with

---

[92] See, for example, Utting, Sir W. B., 1997, *op.cit.*

Barnado's, 1996, *Too Much Too Young: The Failure of Social Policy in Meeting the Needs of Care Leavers,* The Action on Aftercare Consortium.

[93] Colwell, 1974, *Report of the Committee of Inquiry into the Care and Supervision Provided in Relation to Maria Colwell,* HMSO, London.

the welfare of the child or family, but to public lack of confidence in the abilities of social workers to prevent, in particular the death, of children at the hands of their carers. Local authorities, social workers, courts and doctors became increasingly risk averse and increasingly bureaucratic in their attempts to avoid blame.

The irony was that from the late 1970s onwards families lost fiscal and welfare support at a time when the government began to place increasing emphasis on the family's importance. The Labour government of James Callaghan had witnessed the first major drive since the war to reduce welfare expenditure, and the economic austerity that marked the beginning of the Thatcher government led to repeated Ministerial statements stressing the importance of the family as provider and carer to all its members, and as a bulwark against the fecklessness, delinquency and criminality caused by those who did not conform. Lone parents, in particular, were targeted and their entitlement to housing and financial support questioned. Women who did not want the father involved in the child's life, were to have their benefit withdrawn upon failure to disclose his name or whereabouts which would enable the newly formed Child Support Agency to pursue him. The then Prime Minister, Mrs Thatcher, spoke of a return to the good old Victorian values of family life, stressing the importance of marriage and parental responsibility. Like the Victorians, the Thatcher government stressed the importance of individualism, hard work, responsibility and rights that were earned. Those sentiments were to find echo in the Children Act 1989, and in more recent Conservative governments.

The inquiries into the deaths of Jasmine Beckford (London Borough of Brent 1985), Tyra Henry (London Borough of Lambeth 1987), and Kimberley Carlile (London Borough of Greenwich 1987) thus led to criticism of social work policy, practice, knowledge and skills, and as Otway[94]points out, to a perceived need to reformulate the management of the problem at the inter-agency, agency and individual case level. Moreover, social workers were seen as too gullible and trusting of parents, and thus as failing to prioritise the welfare of the child or the protection system. The system finally buckled under the weight of the Cleveland inquiry in 1987.[95] For now, paradoxically, social workers were seen as too judgmental, impetuous and irresponsible in removing children, thought to be the victims of sexual abuse, from their homes under emergency protection orders. The report of the inquiry noted that inter-agency and inter-professional misunderstandings had obscured the need for a child-centred approach, and called for better and more formal inter-agency working in child protection.

Once again, the reformulation was to contain, perhaps, inherent contradictions. The welfare of the child which had, according to the Cleveland inquiry report, been jeopardised by poor interagency working was now to be secured by a system of interagency working and legislative power that, arguably, once again sidelined the welfare of the child. Thus, for example, post Cleveland the relationship between social services and the police changed from a sequential one in which the social worker first investigated and then consulted with the police, to working together with what Kemp (Cleveland conference, 1997)[96]calls 'a high premium being placed on working in agreement with each other's objectives.' The result was to focus police and social services departments on the medical examination and video interviewing of children where assessment indicated that, for example, sexual

94 Otway, O., 1996, *op.cit*, p.157.

95 Cleveland, 1988, *Report of the Inquiry into Child Abuse in Cleveland 1987,* Cmnd. 412, HMSO, London.

96 Kemp, P., 1997, *Lessons for Social Services,* Lecture notes issued at 'Cleveland 10 Years On' conference, 14 April 1997, University of Northumbria at Newcastle.

abuse had taken place, largely regardless of whether a prosecution was likely to follow.[97]

---

[97] Ritchie, C., 1997, *Child Sexual Abuse and the Criminal Justice System,* MSc thesis, University of Oxford.

3. POST 1989

The Children Act 1989 thus came to represent an uneasy alliance between children's and parents' rights following public alarm about the over zealous removal of children from their parents in Cleveland. Although informed by the earlier Economic and Social Research Council and DHSS research on decision making in child care, the report of the Social Services Committee 1984 and the Review of Child Care Law, it was the inquiries that provided the catalyst for change. The Act also had a place within the wider political context of individualism and austerity. Its philosophy, enshrined in the Guidance and Regulations on the 1989 Children Act, volume 2, is that -

> "the best place for the [child] to be brought up is usually
> in the [child's] own family and the [child] in need can be
> helped most effectively if the local authority, working in
> partnership with the parents, provides a range and level of
> services appropriate to the [child's] needs."

Although section 17 set out to 'safeguard and promote the welfare of children' through the provision of supportive services, the very nature of its 'general duty' was to ensure that local authorities had no actual duty to provide support to a particular child. Thus the 1989 Act did not oblige local authorities to support particular children or parents. Rather, through the use of section 47 'at risk' investigations, resources were targeted on child protection.

The strengthening of inter-agency working in the name of protection, whilst not yet on the scale of mandatory reporting found in the United States, may have served to close avenues of support and prevention. Thus the practice guide of the Social Services Inspectorate for 1994 states about someone who has self-referred to the social services -

> "a careful judgement should be made about whether the present danger, or likelihood of harm to the child, requires further enquiries to be made or whether it would suffice to offer assistance under Section 17 of the Children Act 1989 . . . If it becomes obvious that further enquiries under child protection procedures are needed, but child protection issues were not the original concern of the referrer, this is likely to be a distressing development to the person making the referral and she or he may wish to withdraw. The impossibility of this must be explained and every effort should be made to engage the family as positively as possible in the further work."[98]

There are but two options: preventive work under section 17 - if the social worker is *sure* that 'it would suffice' - or further child protection procedures under section 47 of the Children Act 1989. It is impossible for the parent to withdraw if child protection issues arise. Section 17 demands that the social worker takes the risk; section 47 offers the social worker a sharing of the burden, resources and support. Although section 17 empowers local authorities to provide services it does not place a duty on government or local authorities to provide fiscal or individual support. Thus section 47 acts to legitimise resource rationing at a time when public expenditure is still under pressure. As Gibbons, Conroy and Bell noted,[99] register status in the mid 1990s largely determined a family's chances of receiving supportive services.

---

[98] Department of Health, 1994, *The Challenge of Partnership in Child Protection: Practice Guide,* Social Services Inspectorate, HMSO, London.

[99] Gibbons, J., Conroy, S., Bell, C., 1995, *op.cit.*

The language of social work, at least until the mid 1990s, had become the language of 'investigation', 'assessment', 'dangerousness' 'risk' and 'forensic evidence'.The language, as Otway points out,[100] might be seen as more akin not to that of the caring professions but to that of the police. The 1990s saw the end of social workers as counsellors or therapists, and the emergence of case managers, assessing 'risk' within a legalistic framework. It was for the social worker to decide 'risk' and the court to interpret 'is suffering, or is likely to suffer, significant harm'.

Thus the inquiries of the 1970s and 1980s, which culminated in the Children Act 1989, have shaped and still shape our childcare thinking. Lack of research into the numbers of those who, unbeknownst to social services, suffer long-term mental and emotional disabilities as a result of parenting difficulties, combined with a lack of research into the value of care, and alternatives to it, still allows the spotlight to fall on to individual cases and the apparent failings of social workers. By the turn of the last century, child protection was consuming a massive part of the total budget for all interventions for children and young people. At 2014-2015 prices, child protection and safeguarding cost an estimated £6 billion or 36% of the total spend, with over £5 billion of that being spent on looked after children. The cost was to be born by already hard-strapped local authorities. Little wonder then that not enough money was available for the public health approach that the 21st century should have heralded. Little surprise that there is no cash in the pot for the needs of so many of our young people. Little wonder that despite all the money spent, all the procedures and social workers, all the secrecy of our Family Courts, which require that parents do not discuss their

[100] Otway, O., 1996, *op.cit.* p.159
* ChildLine Review: *What has affected children in Aprial 2014-March 2015.* London: NSPCC
* *NSPCC (2013) *How safe are our children?* London: NSPCC
* * https://www.nspcc.org.uk/services-and-resources/research-and-resources/statistics/
* ** Chowdry, H (2016) *The immediate fiscal cost of late intervention for children and young people.* The Early Intervention Foundation

case with the media or with others, all the commissions and inquiries into child deaths and yes, despite the fact that the number of children who die at the hands of their parents has stayed more or less constant for the past 20 years, at a mean of approximately 50 - in 2014, for example, 46 homicide victims were aged under 16[101] - money continues to be poured into child protection.

Bear in mind too, that comparatively little money is spent on protecting children on our streets, and the Department for Transport notes that since 2010, the number of those under 15 who are killed in road traffic accidents has stayed static at between 50-60 per year.[102] A further 46 children under 19 drowned in 2013[103], and between 2012 and 2013, an average of 11 children, under the age of 14, committed suicide.[104]

The paraphernalia of the state, targeted at particular children and families, is a massive cost to the economy, a drain on resources that could otherwise be used for support and prevention, and is ultimately ineffectual. It may improve life for a very few but not for the many who are also vulnerable. It is time that practitioners, academics and others dared to raise their heads from the parapet of risk, and to begin to press for a public health model of child and family welfare, that is inclusive, supportive, universal, accessible and welcomed by parents.

---

[101]Office for National Statistics (2015) *Focus on violent crime and sexual offences.*
http://www.ons.gov.uk/peoplepopulationandcommunity/crimeandjustice/compendium/
focusonviolentcrimeandsexualoffences/2015-02-12/chapter2violentcrimeandsexualoffenceshomicide#victims-aged-under-16-years

[102] Department for Transport (2016) *Reported road casualties in Great Britain: main results 2015.* Statistical Release 30 June 2016

[103] RoSPA (2013) http://www.rospa.com/media-centre/press-office/press-releases/detail/?id=1276

[104] Scowcroft, E (2016) *Suicide statistics report 2016.* London: The Samaritans

KEY POINTS

1. Our current model of child protection and the placement of children in
    care is rooted in a Victorian model that focused solely on the poor.

2. Care homes, fostering and adoption continue a practice that is long
outdated.

3. Time and again inquiries have reported the abuse rife in care homes, yet
little has changed.

4. The current focus on risk or safeguarding consumes resources and finances
that might actually be used to support children and families in need.

5. Despite the inquiries, changes in practice and increased numbers in care,
the number of child homicides over the past 20 years has remained more or
less constant.

Questions for Discussion

(a) To what extent is the current model of child protection based on a male
dominated view of parenting and care that ignores the needs of primary
carers (usually mothers) and fails to involve or target fathers?

(b) To what extent do the NSPCC, Barnardos, the Children's Society and
Action for Children continue to influence policy and practice, and how do
their salaries, pensions and expenditure (available to view on the Charity
Commission website - click on accounts) compare with the incomes of
those they serve?

(c) With reference to children's charities' marketing and image use, to what extent are these charities in the business of marketing children rather than parental or family need?

(d) To what extent does a focus on individual children and 'risk' take attention away from the real killers, such as road traffic, obesity or lack of physical fitness?

CHAPTER TWO

THE KNOWN TRIGGERS FOR CHILD DEATHS AND INFANTICIDES

The number of children who sadly die at their parents' hands has scarcely changed over recent decades, whilst the number of those in care has on the whole risen over the past 70 years. Repeated attempts to tighten up child protection or safeguarding have not led to any real improvement in the critical criteria of reducing child deaths or numbers in care.

England and Wales do not have one identifiable way of recording child homicides by family perpetrator, and statistics in this area vary depending on how they have been measured. Since 2008 Local Safeguarding Children Boards in England have been required to set up a child death review process for all child deaths (homicides, natural causes, road accidents etc). The Child Death Overview Panels review each child death in their area and publish annual reports for year ending 31 March. It is by no means a perfect way of recording child homicides by family members, as it does not actually record whether a family member committed the homicide, but it gives some idea of number of child homicides and continuity. The figures below are taken from the Department for Education's child death reviews for the years available: 2010-2017.[105]

[105] https://www.gov.uk/government/collections/statistics-child-death-reviews, accessed 20/11/17

Year ending 31 March all children 0 - 18 years	Number recorded in England as dying from 'deliberately inflicted injury/abuse or neglect or 'apparent homicide'	Number of looked after children, reported in Department for Education Statistical releases*
2010	30	64,400
2011	47	65,520
2012	26	67,050
2013	30	68,110
2014	48	68,840
2015	46	69,540
2016	32	70,440
2017	36	72,670

*https://www.gov.uk/government/uploads/system/uploads/
attachment_data/file/218974/sfr27-2010v2.pdf

Moreover, there is no evidence that care improves lives for the majority, and some evidence that it makes their lives worse, and perpetuates cycles of life in care.

In terms of risk, a fatality that social services might have been 'responsible' for is what every local authority seeks to avoid. It is not just the individual life; it is the fear that has become synonymous with managing children's services. Thus much of the edifice of child protection is based on that underlying theme; the worst case scenario. From time to time the sheer horror and bewildering lack of intervention arouse particular media and professional interest. Cases such as Khyra Ishaq and Daniel Pelka, who both died of starvation in 2010 and 2012 respectively, or Ayeeshia Jane Smith, who died from a tear to the heart in May 2014 caused by her mother, naturally attract media attention. Social work practice in relation to children 'at risk' received UK-wide attention following the death of Baby P (Lord Laming, 2009) and three serious case reviews in Doncaster into infant deaths in 2004, 2006 and 2007. Following the death of Baby P and the removal of the Director of

Children's Services, Sharon Shoesmith, many practitioners signed petitions and wrote on Community Care blogs, deploring the scapegoating of social workers, whilst the media focused on the appalling suffering that had gone unnoticed. Yet as if paralysed by fear of criticism from the media, policy makers failed to respond in a reasoned and evidence-based way to the plight both of child protection teams and families. The Laming Report (2009) offered insights and constructive approaches towards reducing risk, but did not set out - nor was it within its scope - to bring about reasoned change to both policy and practice. The time for that is now long overdue.

Now is the time to think the unthinkable, to remove the focus from risk/ safeguarding and protection and to turn it towards open access and universal support, underpinned by a public health strategy that promotes the wellbeing of all children and families.

But adopting this approach, we need first to see what the real risks are. A report by Unicef (2003:4) placed the UK as the 6th 'best' nation in terms of child deaths from maltreatment in OECD countries. It is noticeable that the countries whose practices (perhaps because they are English speaking) we often cite as laudable, perform very poorly in the Unicef table: the USA (second to bottom/27th), Canada (20th), Australia (21st) and New Zealand (25th) all have notably worse child maltreatment death rates than the United Kingdom despite the fact that they have arguably more 'evolved' child protection systems that include, in the case of the USA, Canada and Australia, mandatory reporting.[106]

---

[106] eg. In the USA, all States, the District of Columbia, American Samoa, Guam, the Northern Mariana Islands, Puerto Rico, and the U.S. Virgin Islands have statutes identifying persons who are required to report suspected child maltreatment to an appropriate agency. Each year approximately 1 in 16 families are affected. https://en.m.wikipedia.org/wiki/Mandatory_reporting_in_the_United_States, accessed 9/11/2017

Although the UK performs relatively well in terms of infanticide, there is no room for complacency. A public health approach notes that a key factor underpinning positions in the Unicef league table for child maltreatment deaths are rates of poverty. A more recent Unicef report (2007:4) identified the UK as the worst economically advanced country in terms of child well-being. Out of the 21 countries with sufficient data for analysis, the UK came 18th in terms of child material deprivation, and bottom for 'family and peer relationships' and for 'behaviours and risks' just one below the USA. At the top of the scale for child well-being came the Netherlands, followed by Sweden, Denmark, Finland, Spain, Switzerland and Norway (Unicef 2007:4). Moreover, child well-being in the UK has been highlighted as particularly bad given the national level of wealth.[107]

What the Unicef reports (2003; 2007) make clear is that the UK suffers from a lack of social cohesion, underpinned by poverty and by the inexorable gap between rich and poor, which particularly impacts children (ONS 2016; Hood and Waters 2017)[108]. Despite initiatives to improve the fabric of social life, there remain – as any practitioner will attest – gaps in services, staffing and provision, particularly at a time of austerity. It is not the fault of social workers that so many citizens live below the poverty threshold, nor that so many of them are unable to access - as a universal right, without the need of a broker - the services that they need to improve their parenting environment and capacity. Social workers know this; they experience it every day. It is more than 20 years since the publication of the seminal work, Child

[107] Bradshaw J and Richardson D (2009) *An index of child well-being in Europe.* http://www.york.ac.uk/inst/spru/research/unicef/EU29.pdf, accessed 7/9/2016

[108] Hood A and Waters T (2017) Living standards, poverty and inequality in the UK: 2016–17 to 2021–22. Institute of Fiscal Studies: JRF
https://www.jrf.org.uk/report/living-standards-poverty-and-inequality-uk-2016-17-2021-22
Office for National Statistics (2016) Statistical bulletin:
Household disposable income and inequality in the UK: financial year ending 2016.
https://www.ons.gov.uk/peoplepopulationandcommunity/personalandhouseholdfinances/incomeandwealth/bulletins/householddisposableincomeandinequality/financialyearending2016

Protection: Messages from Research (Department of Health, 1995) which called for an end to the rationing of services to children in need and their families. For it is not only the children, but also (as the Children Act s.17 makes clear) their families who need to be able to access the support and services that they need. The dominant austerity agenda of sequential goverments from 2010 has meant ever fewer resources for the expanding child population.

So what are the triggers for child deaths, and could they be mitigated through public health strategies? Brandon et al (2008) reported on findings from serious case reviews, and noted that where parents were involved –

> 'There is evidence that domestic violence is present
> in two thirds of the cases (66%), substance misuse in 57%, and
> mental ill health in 55% of families ' – (Brandon et al, 2008:51)

These three: domestic violence, substance misuse and mental health difficulties, are all factors that can be dealt with by public health policy initiatives.
If we add into the mix that almost half of 16 year old looked after children have been identified by Meltzer et al (2004) as having a mental disorder, that 11% of care leavers have problematic alcohol or drug use, and that in one study, half of young people in children's homes had substance misuse problems,[109] we can see that regardless whether they might also have been damaged if left at home, care has certainly not proved successful.

---

[109] Home Office (2003) *One problem amongst many: drug use amongst careleavers in transition to independent living.* London: Home Office
Department for Education (2012) *Outcomes for children looked after by local authorities in England.* London: DoE

Mental Health and Risk in the General Population

Of course depression and psychosis can have an impact on a parent's ability to cope and awareness of the importance of treating mental and physical illness equally is now growing. Most parents manage but for a small percentage of parents, proactive help is needed. Serious psychiatric disturbance is a factor in about 30% of fatal child abuse.[110] The risk was first identified by Steele and Pollock (1968) who, using a sample of predominantly affluent parents, identified a link between poor mental health and the possibility of abuse. If we consider that more affluent parents are more likely to obtain the required treatment from their doctors (Hart 1971),[111] are more likely to be able to access other therapies, are more able to use nannies/au pairs/babysitters, are more likely to be better educated around the issues affecting parenting and are known to suffer fewer life stressors we can see that they themselves are able to reduce risk. They have agency. For low income parents, and care leavers, high quality mental health support that links with children's services is still largely absent (Mental Health Act Commission 2005; Street and Svanberg 2003, The Guardian 2016).[112]

More recently (Hogg 2015)[113] has called for far greater perinatal mental health support, identifying that 73% of maternity services do not have a specialist mental health midwife, that 64% of Clinical Commissioning Groups did not have a perinatal mental health strategy and that half of mental health trusts do not have a perinatal mental health service with a specialist psychiatrist. The report concludes that –

---

[110]Department of Health (2008) Department of Health (2008) *Care programme approach briefing: parents with mental health problems and their children.* http://www.scie.org.uk/publications/guides/guide30/files/CPAbriefing.pdf?res=true

[111]Hart, JT (1971). "The Inverse Care Law". Lancet. 1: 405–12. doi:10.1016/s0140-6736(71)92410-x.

[112] 1. Ment Health Today. 2003 Jul-Aug:28-30. Listening to young people. Street C, Svanberg J. PMID: 14625917 https://www.theguardian.com/commentisfree/2016/oct/24/mental-health-children-camhs-jeremy-hunt-nhs-tragedies-funding-cuts

[113] Hogg S (2015) *Prevention in Mind.* London: NSPCC

'If we are to significantly reduce the harm caused by perinatal mental illness in England, a significant change is needed in our universal services ... Mental health needs to be given parity of esteem with physical health in the work of primary care services.' (Hogg 2015, p.3)

Moreover, antenatal and perinatal professionals tend to see the mothers, rather than the fathers, and to assume that mood disorders and schizophrenia or psychosis pose the highest risk, whereas research (Flynn et al 2013)[114] suggests that, for example, parental psychosis is not as great a risk for infanticide as personality disorder, and we know that fathers kill more children than mothers. It is therefore key that if risk to young children is to be reduced, more research into parental mental illness, antenatal and perinatal support and access to services is needed, and that research must also includes fathers.

One star on the horizon is the Family Nurse Partnership programme, which is available in England but which has to be commissioned by individual local authorities, and which is not yet universal. Based on research in the USA (Olds et al 1986)[115] and with pilots already evaluated here,[116] it provides midwife one-to-one support to mothers under 20 (nothing in particular for

---

[114] Flynn, S. M., Shaw, J. J., & Abel, K. M. (2013). Filicide: Mental Illness in Those Who Kill Their Children. PLoS ONE, 8(4), [e58981]. DOI: 10.1371/journal.pone.0058981. Publication link: b1b33ca1-39d2-445a-8c51-fc634fb6e3a5

[115] DL, Henderson CR Jr, Tatelbaum R, Chamberlin R.Improving the delivery of prenatal care and outcomes of pregnancy: a randomized trial of nurse home visitation. *Journal of Pediatrics* 1986 Jul;78(1):138

[116] https://www.gov.uk/government/uploads/system/uploads/attachment_data/file/216864/The-Family-Nurse-Partnership-Programme-Information-leaflet.pdf
https://www.nice.org.uk/guidance/ph40/documents/social-and-emotional-wellbeing-early-years-expert-report-42
http://fnp.nhs.uk/sites/default/files/contentuploads/fnp_information_pack_-_the_evidence_for_fnp_-_appendix_11.pdf
Robbing M et al (2014, amended 2015) *The building blocks trial.* Department of Health Research Programme Project

fathers) from early pregnancy until the child is aged two, thus allowing young mothers to explore emotional, physical, educational and practical needs with a professional with no fear of judgement but with easy on demand access. Having interviewed many of its recipients, it is clear that the programme is non-stigmatising, supportive, educative and well-received. Health visitors come to know their clients very well, and in turn the young mothers feel able to ask questions, reveal difficulties and explore the needs of their growing infant in a safe and supportive environment. It may not be a panacea, and research suggests that where parents have identifiable mental health issues, extra support may be needed,[117] but it is a cause for cautious optimism.

It is known from serious case reviews, that a critical period both for maternal self harm, and infanticide, is the first few weeks after release from hospital, when the parent is back in the home and may again experience mental health issues. Depression and suicidal ideation can lead parents to kill their children in the belief that they can be better together in death, and a psychotic mother or father may believe that they are saving their children from a traumatic but imagined event by killing them. Others may suffer from auditory hallucinations that 'command' them to act. Research suggests (Hatters et al 2007)[118] that just as we now ask the 'suicide question' when someone is depressed, GPs, counsellors and those working in mental health also need to ask, 'Have you had any thoughts about harming the children'. To ask that question and to expect an honest answer, also requires the parent to feel safe to give that answer. They must not feel that their children will be taken from them. If necessary, the parent may spend time out of the home whilst other support is placed in the home; something that to most would not only be

---

[117] Schrader-McMillan A, Barnes J and Barlow J (2012) *Primary study evidence on the effectiveness of interventions (home, early education, child care) in promoting the social and emotional wellbeing of vulnerable children under 5.* https://www.nice.org.uk/guidance/ph40/documents/social-and-emotional-wellbeing-early-years-expert-report-12

[118] Hatters MLA, Friedman S and Resnick P (2007). "Child Murder by Mothers: Patterns and Prevention." *World Psychiatry* 6.3 (2007): 137–141. Print.
https://www.ncbi.nlm.nih.gov/pmc/articles/PMC2174580/

acceptable, but welcomed. Yet currently fears about child protection hinder rather than encourage honesty, as this extract from the Department of Health's own research shows -.

> 'Parents say that they appreciate additional support when they are unwell.[119]Parents describe how they fear losing their children, and the reality of it happening.[120]They feel on trial about their parenting abilities[121]and though they may need help, they fear the consequences of asking for it. Women are frightened to come forward for help, particularly black women.'[122]

Despite the above quote from the Department of Health and how it screams for support, the emphasis is on the risk to the children, which in turn inhibits parents from opening up. This, despite the fact that between 30% and 50% of those who use mental health services are parents.[123]

Tailoring services to meet parents' needs is therefore critical. Where a parent has been in crisis, it is vital to have a support package that works. For example, to know whether a parent has relapsed following hospitalisation requires regular contact by someone the parent trusts in that critical period following release, when the parent is once again faced with the multiple

---

[119] Robinson B and Scott S (2007) *Parents in hospital: how mental health services can best promote family contact when a parent is in hospital,* Barnardo

[120] Hugman R and Phillips N (1993) *Like bees round the honeypot: social work responses to parents with mental health needs.* Practice 6(3)

[121] Darton K, Gorman UJ and Sayce L (1994) *Eve fights back,* Mind Publications

[122] Quote from Department of Health (2008) *Care programme approach briefing: parents with mental health problems and their children.* http://www.scie.org.uk/publications/guides/guide30/files/CPAbriefing.pdf?res=true

[123] Department of Health (2008) *Care programme approach briefing: parents with mental health problems and their children.* http://www.scie.org.uk/publications/guides/guide30/files/CPAbriefing.pdf?res=true

stressors of home. In theory the care programme approach,[124] or enhanced care programme for those considered a risk to themselves or others, means that parents with higher risk will be assessed, will be linked into other agencies and have regular contact their care worker. However, for the reasons discussed above, their real needs will probably not be expressed for fear of the consequences for their children.

Many people will for one reason or another feel dissatisfied, rightly or wrongly with the service they receive, yet although they can request change, they are not agents. They cannot choose how they want to be supported or who their clinician is, even at critical points, because they are *receiving* a service; not purchasing it as their wealthier counterparts might do. Rethink, a mental health charity, for example, suggests that such a person might –

> 'be able to resolve these problems by talking to [their] care co-ordinator or with the team manager. An advocate might be able to help you with this. You could try searching for local advocacy services on line.'[125]

When a vulnerable parent has to search online for someone to help them at such a critical point in their lives, policy needs to change.

Finally, one of the biggest lacuna in NHS provision for mental illness is the lack of ability to self admit to hospital with support in the home for other children being put in place, and the lack of immediate and ongoing daily support on discharge. We have known for years that many infanticides and

---

[124] The Care Programme Approach is a package of care used by secondary mental health services. It should be available to those with needs from different services or those thought to be a high risk. It should include a care plan and someone to coordinate care. All care plans must include a crisis plan.

[125] https://www.rethink.org/resources/c/care-programme-approach-cpa-factsheet

parental suicides occur shortly after a parent has been discharged from hospital. Research by MBRRACE-UK (2015)[126], which again focused on mothers alone, found that almost a quarter of women who died between 6 weeks and one year after pregnancy, died from mental health related causes, and one seventh from suicide. Whilst the report calls for more attention to be given to the signs and symptoms expressed by this group of women, or for NHS staff to improve their knowledge base, it still adopts a gatekeeping approach, which demands that parents go first to the GP and so on. For many, that is one step too far. They need help now, when they want it, and they should be able to access it on demand, free of stigma, and with in-home funded support provided, if necessary, whilst they are in hospital or ill.

Whilst the Maternal Mental Health alliance and Family Nurse Partnerships can strive to improve outcomes for parents with mental illness, they alone are not enough. Unless and until the National Health Service is dedicated to proper mental health support, which includes a right to be hospitalised on demand, a right to access a mother and baby unit and sufficient provision of such units, a right to in-home support whilst hospitalised, a right to ongoing support with a peer mental health worker, that risk to children and to their parents will continue. Moreover, such support is cost effective. The PSSRU (Bauer et al 2016)[127] reported that post natal depression, anxiety and psychosis carried a total long-term cost of £8.1 billion for each one year cohort of births in the UK, and that 72% of that cost related to adverse impacts on the child rather than the mother. Care is not the answer; universal support and a public health approach is.

[126] MMBRACE (2015) *Surveillance of maternal deaths in the UK 2011-2013 and lessons to be learned to inform maternity care from the UK and Ireland confidential inquiries into maternal deaths and morbidity 2009-2013.* National Perinatal Epidemiology Unit. University of Oxford.

[127] Bauer A et al (2016) *The costs of perinatal mental health problems.* LSE: PSSRU

Substance Misuse and Child Deaths

What do we say about a parent who is apparently reported to continually use drugs, and even snort his own father's ashes mixed with cocaine? What do we say about a father who drinks before lunch and before supper, usually spirits and usually doubles? The first, Keith Richard, [128]may have gone briefly to prison for possession, but was not the subject of child protection investigations and has apparently well adjusted now adult children. The second is my own father; a lovelier man it would be hard to find.

This is not to make light of addictions, but to emphasise that the effect of them can be very much mediated by other protective/resilience factors in the child's life; not the least of which is relative affluence. A parent who has to steal to fund a habit, who cannot provide enough food on the table, who leaves dangerous drugs or equipment such as needles where small children can find them, who doesn't have an au pair or nanny to look after the children, needs practical support. In an ideal world, they will be motivated to end their addiction, but in the meantime real and practical support, including support in the home, can be essential.

Parents who are addicted to drugs are also more likely to be emotionally unavailable to their children. Every year about 100,000 parents or adults living with children in the home will be treated for drug abuse and of them, approximately 11,000 will be parents.[129]Parents who live with their children tend to have fewer problems, be on less harmful drugs, and are in general easier to treat. Each year about 1,000 women entering treatment will be pregnant. Parents who do not have the care of their children tend to be on

---

[128] https://en.m.wikipedia.org/wiki/Keith_Richards

[129] National Treatment Agency for Substance Misuse (2015) *Parents with drug problems: how treatment helps families.* http://www.nta.nhs.uk/uploads/families2012vfinali.pdf

Class A drugs such as heroin, or crack cocaine, and are less likely to complete treatment (approximately one third complete on average).[130]The National Treatment Agency for Substance Misuse report (2015) notes that using the joint Guidance (NTA/DfE), some parts of the country are working well and linking treatment with family support such as health visitors, Sure Start, children's charities, counselling and parenting help, but the same report also notes (page 6) -

> 'Parents who have had their children removed are likely to have serious and complex problems that are difficult to overcome, and it may take them several attempts to recover from drug addiction. They could also lack the strong motivating factor of living with children and may not be getting family related support'.[131]

There can be no doubt that it is vital to ensure that children of drug abusing parents are fully supported and networked into local services, but removing them from the home should not be done without an holistic assessment that balances the needs of parents and children against the services that can be offered. Many local authorities will do this, but the planning for, and availability of services for children, and the overriding concern for the child's welfare, often means the 'easier' path is taken, with the child removed into care.

The most obvious danger to small infants comes either from accidentally smothering a baby who is sharing the same bed, or from alcohol or drug fuelled violence. The former is relatively rare, and certainly far fewer infants die in this way than are killed by road traffic accidents. The latter is linked to domestic violence and requires that a cycle of abuse is ended.

---

[130] All figures, NTASA, *op cit*

[131] NTASA (2015) *op cit.* page 6

Substance abuse and perpetrator violence/filicide has been linked to perpetrator experience of emotional abuse as a child in particular, but also to experiencing physical abuse and exposure to parental violence, as a child.[132] We know that previous maltreatment is a good indicator of later behavioural problems, including aggression, abusive behaviour, alcohol and drug misuse.[133] We also know that taking children into care does not seem to modify or improve these outcomes. Public health initiatives, however, aimed at improving and enabling parenting can change outcomes. A precursor to accepting help, is understanding that you need it. This insight can sometimes only be gained by using mass and social media to get the message across: modelling our own parents' behaviour is never good enough. As the Faculty of Public Health at the Royal College of Physicians notes, targeted parenting classes will often miss the very parents who need help most. In general, universal open access parenting groups, which involve parents in a bottom up, rather than top down approach are more likely to be successful.

There are many parenting programmes, the majority of which emanate from the USA and involve some degree of expense. But as has been noted -

> 'Optimal parenting requires warmth, affection, sensitivity, empathy, honesty, encouragement and creation of opportunities for learning, as well as clear, consistent, age-appropriate boundaries enforced by positive discipline

---

[132] Eriksson L et al (2016) Maternal and paternal filicide: Case studies from the Australian Homicide Project. *Child Abuse Review. 25 (17-30).* http://onlinelibrary.wiley.com/store/10.1002/car.2358/asset/car2358.pdf;jsessionid=485744E38CC6A7773079BAD0878615CF.f01t04?v=1&t=iubcjf7q&s=86824880771888c0909ed6c70682e65c158a7a2e. *Accessed 15/10/2016*

[133] See, for example, Day C et al (2014) *A literature review into child abuse and/or neglect prior to custody:* Youth Justice Board

(eg. praising good behaviour and ignoring bad), problem
solving and conflict resolution skills.'[134]

These are skills which may not be possessed but can be learned. The Family
Nurse Partnership scheme can promote much of this antenatally and through
to age two. These are the key years both for the child's experience and for
parental bonding. In two more years' time, the child will be at school, and the
deficiencies inherent in poor parenting will be making themselves felt in
emotional and behavioural difficulties, school exclusion and later
unemployment. A vicious cycle that can be broken not by placing the child in
care, where he is separated from those he loves, placed among frequently low
achieving and temporary staff, with few of his support networks, if any,
available, but by supporting and enabling parents from antenatal through to
the school gates and beyond. Sure Start and Children's Centres have made a
start, but they are vulnerable to local authority funding cuts/closure and tend
to operate in the poorer neighbourhoods. They are also linked into the very
services, such as social work, that some parents fear. Smaller more universal
services/centres that offer real choice of venue and relinquish their concerns
with child protection can offer a real way forward to exploring positive
parenting, reducing violence and moderating substance misuse and its effects.

Dual diagnosis

Dual diagnosis occurs when a person has both mental health and substance
abuse problems, aggravating the effectiveness of any medication and
increasing the likelihood of psychotic and delusional states. Some parents
may use drugs such as cannabis to self medicate for less severe mental health
problems or for physical pain, with possibly positive effects, but where more
severe mental health and drug use are simultaneously involved, there is

---

[134] Stewart Brown, S (2006) *Parenting and public health.* Faculty of Public Health (RCP) Briefing
Statement

clearly increased risk for children. However, this risk should not be overstated. The percentage of parents with dual diagnosis is unknown, but the prevalence of dual diagnosis in the general adult population in the UK is estimated to be between 0.05% and 0.16%[135]. Service provision is patchy, and a systematic review of community health and social care services in 2015 found:

> 'The review of current service configuration for adults and young people with dual diagnosis was marked by its lack of any coherent national framework or structure, in spite of consensus agreements on key elements of treatment approaches, most notably the Department of Health (2002) Good Practice Guide'. [136]

Whilst political parties may currently favour more much needed expenditure on mental health services, the same report notes that there also needs to be a synthesising of health and social care and a national reorganisation of services if they are to meet this group's needs.

Although there is no evidence that parental dual diagnosis is prevalent within infanticide figures, it is a cause for concern. Currently, a parent must self refer to their GP before obtaining access to any dual diagnosis or community mental health teams in their area. It is this first hurdle that so many find too risky or too daunting to overcome. Self referral that does not involve the 'authorities' (such as the independent and private facilities used by their wealthier counterparts) whilst at first appearing more risky to children, may in fact produce a safer environment for them. Even then, parents are only too well aware that where children are involved, such facilities may involve social

[135] Megnin-Viggars O, Brown M, Marcus E, Stockton S and Pilling P (2015) *Draft Mental Illness and Substance Misuse (Dual Diagnosis) Community Health and Social Care Services.* NICE, p.10

[136] Megnin-Viggars O, et al (op cit). p.100

workers and other health professionals with 'safeguarding' obligations, and this may frequently be a barrier to seeking help.

In 2016, the vice chair of the British Association of Social Workers pointed out in Community Care, that since 1996 child protection investigations and assessments had climbed inexorably upwards, and now accounted for one in 20 families in England and Wales. Her point is that social work with families is 'increasingly about mutual distrust and fear.'[137]Since the Children Act 1989, she points out that referrals and assessments have both tripled and reiterates the point that -

> 'Despite there being no significant rise in the number
> of children who die as a result of parental abuse or
> neglect, risk of abuse is assumed to be high.'[138]

Parents who are already living with the blight of poverty, stress and poor housing, can see social work not as a support, but as a threat. So in this key area of dual diagnosis, where it is vital that help is sought, the biggest barrier to receiving it is that age-old natural instinct to protect your children from outsiders; outsiders whom they know will make them the object of disempowering assessments and referrals. The social worker may be excellent in reality, but no parent wants to make themselves vulnerable if they can possibly manage not to.

Domestic Violence

As we have seen (Brandon et al 2008), the prevalence of domestic violence in infanticides is estimated at 66%. Every three days a woman or a mother is

[137] *Community Care,* February 19th 2016, Have parents become the enemy in social work? http://www.communitycare.co.uk/2016/02/19/parents-become-enemy-social-work/

[138] *Community Care,* February 19th 2016, Have parents become the enemy in social work? http://www.communitycare.co.uk/2016/02/19/parents-become-enemy-social-work/

killed in England and Wales (ONS2015), 20% of children in the UK have been exposed to domestic abuse (Radford et al. NSPCC, 2011). in 90% of domestic violence incidents in family households, children were in the same or the next room (Hughes, 1992) and 62% of children in households where domestic violence is happening are also directly harmed (SafeLives, 2015).[139] Taking children out of the home is not the answer; preventing domestic violence and/or removing the abuser is.

The European Union Agency for Fundamental Rights[140] data for 2012 shows how prevalent domestic violence is in northern Europe in particular, and notably in the UK (29%) , Finland (30%), and Sweden (28%). Data for Denmark, shows that a staggering 52% of women reported being violently abused at some point in their lives.[141] It is arguable that the northern Europeans are more willing to talk about, and report domestic violence, but nevertheless notable that countries such as Spain, recently recovering from recession and no longer the Catholic country it once was, and Ireland, a close neighbour, appear to perform so much better. That said, recent evidence suggests that Spanish women are only just beginning to speak out about domestic violence, with a recent survey[142] finding that 65% of victims were not employed and that 81% of women thought that financial independence was the key to ending abuse - in other words, the ability to leave a relationship or home.

---

[139] http://www.refuge.org.uk/get-help-now/what-is-domestic-violence/domestic-violence-the-facts/ accessed 9/10/2016

[140] http://fra.europa.eu/sites/default/files/fra-2014-vaw-survey-factsheet_en.pdf Accessed 9/10/16

[141] http://kvinfo.org/web-magazine/are-danish-women-most-abused-women-europe

[142] Adecco Foundation 2012, reported in El Pais http://elpais.com/elpais/2015/11/25/inenglish/ 1448449401_599926.html, accessed 8/10/2016

Another reason given for failure to report domestic violence is that prosecution may lead to loss of employment and therefore income. Add to this growing evidence that abusers not only use their power to control physically and emotionally, but also financially, and we can see the importance of women's financial independence. We know that many women do not leave relationships because they have no access to funds, no financial awareness, and nowhere to go.

A public health initiative, therefore, might require that banks no longer accept joint accounts, that all children learn, not trigonometry at 13, but the real mathematical world of finance, accounts, debt, credit, interest rates, tax and self sufficiency. A more controversial initiative, aimed at ensuring that parenting is not unpaid and undervalued, might be to legislate for fathers, whether or not married or living with the mother, to have to pay a universally set percentage of their income to the mother of any of their children, or vice versa.

Clearly domestic violence often involves psychological control, but when women (or men) want to leave, at a time when they are at their most vulnerable, often with young children and no money, the state needs to enable them. In the rented sector, where families or couples are housed, it should be possible to ensure that sole tenancy agreements are not allowed, thus ensuring that the victim has at least an equal right to reside in the property and obviating some of the need for Court orders. That said, whilst Occupation Orders and Domestic Violence Protection Notices can also help, we may also need to consider expanding the role of women's refuges, to provide more temporary accommodation. Current UK provision of refuge spaces falls short of the Council of Europe's recommended levels, and Women's Aid (2017)[143]

---

[143] Women's Aid (2017) Nowhere to turn: Findings from the first year of the 'No woman turn away project'. https://1q7dqy2unor827bqjls0c4rn-wpengine.netdna-ssl.com/wp-content/uploads/2017/07/NWTA-Executive-Summary-Final.pdf

reports that 45% of survivors could not find any spaces available. The law is necessarily sometimes slow and difficult to enforce; the vulnerable cannot wait. But again, this is not a reason to place children in care; it's a reason to streamline and make more effective our responses to domestic violence. And that includes making counselling available to children of violent parents, so that they can explore issues of control and conflict resolution, thereby avoiding repetition in successive generations.

KEY POINTS

1. There is no evidence that placing children in care reduces the incidence of familial child homicides.
2. There is no evidence that placing children in care improves their life chances or well-being or that of their parents.
3. There is an urgent need to shift the focus from child protection and 'safeguarding' to universal support underpinned by a public health strategy that promotes the well-being of all children and families.
4. Likely triggers for child homicides are domestic violence, substance misuse and mental illness, all of which can be reduced by public health initiatives.
5. Parents need agency so that, like their better off counterparts, they can choose how their issue is resolved without fear of child protection.

QUESTIONS FOR DISCUSSION

a) Is there any evidence that child protection works for children and parents, and what would that evidence look like?
b) Why do the Netherlands, Sweden, Denmark and Finland all do so much better than the UK in terms of child well-being?

c) What would a public health approach to domestic violence look like, and how might men be involved?
d) Whilst substance abuse amongst parents is relatively low, it is a matter of concern. What public health initiatives might better support these parents and their children?

CHAPTER 3

IS PLACING A CHILD IN CARE THE SOLUTION?

The revolving door of risk posed by placing children in care

The same report (Brandon et al, 2008:45) also found that 30% of infanticidal mothers had an experience of care. Acheson (1998) reminded us that a disproportionately high number of girls leave care as mothers or pregnant, and that a high proportion also leave with alcohol or substance abuse problems. We have long known that women who have experienced care, are vulnerable to partnering men who are more likely to increase, rather than reduce risk (Rutter and Quinton 1984; Rutter 1989). In addition, about a quarter of care leavers are pregnant or have a child, and within 18 to 24 months of leaving care that proportion increases (Biehal et al 1995) at the same time as they experience a radical increase in stressors such as independent living, isolation, depression and anxiety (Scott and Hill 2006). Interestingly, the report by Brandon et al (2008) makes no mention of the men/fathers in the study, and it seems in general that their provenance is of no interest.

There is then no evidence that taking children into care saves lives. It may save some, it may cut short the lives of others. There is certainly very little research on the effect on parents, their mental health or lifespan after losing their children into care. But these are matters for further research. The consideration here is that not only does care[144] not appear to work, but it also increases risk not only to the child within it, but for future generations.

When the headlines are not full of the tragic deaths of young children, they are full of on-going accusations of child abuse, made by those who were once

---

[144] 'Care' in this context is taken to mean 'in care' rather than being the subject of a Care Order.

in care. They had been taken away from their families, often from the areas in which they had family connections, and placed largely with staff, many of whom lacked even basic qualification. Little has changed. In 2015, Ofsted advertised the new qualifications needed to work in residential child care - Leadership and Management for Residential Child Care. A diploma is needed at either the top level to manage (5) or the lesser level (3), but to take either diploma requires no prior learning or qualifications (OCR 2016).[145] This, despite the fact that staff are working with some of the most damaged and troubled children in the UK. Those who wish to abuse children can easily access them, just as long as they haven't yet had a conviction.

The same is not true elsewhere in Europe. In Germany, for example, far fewer children are looked after by Court Order, and where they are in children's homes, the majority are encouraged to have regular daily or weekly contact with parents, who in turn are supported by staff in order to improve their parenting. In terms of qualification, in Germany frontline care home staff are trained graduates in social pedagogy, social work or in childhood studies.[146] Such high levels of qualification are commonplace in other countries, eg. Sweden or Norway. Not only do more highly qualified and educated staff bring professionalism but they also bring greater stability and arguably less risk of offending behaviour. In England and Wales, police checks will be made before anyone can work with these vulnerable young people, but many offenders have never actually been convicted, and the very victims that they need: young, vulnerable children, can be accessed relatively easily in an environment which requires very little by way of qualification. This in turn requires scrutiny. We know that sexual abuse in particular, of boys and girls,

[145] http://www.ocr.org.uk/qualifications/vocational-qualifications-qcf-leadership-and-management-for-residential-childcare-england-level-5-diploma-10406/, accessed 23/10/16

[146] Ellis G (2012) International children's homes models: What is transerable to the UK?. Fellowship Report: Winston Churchill Memorial Trust. http://www.wcmt.org.uk/sites/default/files/migrated-reports/1025_1.pdf, accessed 23/10/2106

is more likely to be committed by men,[147] and that children in care are relatively easy prey. It may be time, then, that we considered female only institutional care until a child reaches the age of, for example, 14.

This chapter does not have space to cite the huge number of known cases of abuse in care. There are the infamous, such as Frank Beck, who sexually abused boys in the Leicestershire care homes over which he had authority. There are the almost commonplace examples of the systematic physical and sexual abuse of children in homes, such as Kendall House, Wisteria Lodge, Nottinghamshire, Haut de la Garenne in Jersey, Pindown, Rochdale, Bristol and Derby. There are the cases that are still, in one form or another continuing, such as the widespread sexual and other abuse of children in care in Wales, which led to a number of inquiries. [148]

A conspicuous feature of the abuse of children in care, is the way in which such issues have been repeatedly covered up[149]. The Jillings report into abuse of children in care homes in North Wales, for example, was taken out of public circulation. But the one copy of the Jillings report that seems to have survived[150] found a care system in which the physical and sexual abuse of the children in care was rife. The attempts to hush up the report, by those in power, including by the council's insurance company, led the then Chair of Clwyd (who had been threatened with the sack by the same insurers if he spoke out), to say that the suppression of the Jillings report meant that lessons had not been learned. 'It was the exchange of financial safety for the

---

[147] Radford L, Corral S, Bradley C, Fisher H, Bassett C, Howat N and Collishaw S (2014) *Child abuse and neglect in the UK today.* NSPCC
University of Michigan (2017) *Sexual assault prevention and awareness centre briefing.* https://sapac.umich.edu/article/196

[148] For example, the Utting (1991, Warner (1992) and Waterhouse Report (1994) *Lost in Care*

[149] For example, North Wales, the former Rochdale MP Cyril Smith (http://www.telegraph.co.uk/news/2017/10/09/mi5-knew-cover-up-cyril-smith-child-abuse-inquiry-hears/), Haut de la Garenne in Jersey, Smyllum Park Lanarkshire.

[150] https://en.m.wikipedia.org/wiki/North_Wales_child_abuse_scandal, accessed 25/10/16

safety of real people. It was one of the most shameful parts of recent history'.[151]

There are other cases of abuse that hit the headlines: the young people in Rotherham who were subjected to abuse in their hundreds (Jay 2014)[152]. In Oxford the abuse of an estimated 370 children by a group of males, some already convicted as a result of Operation Bullfinch by the police, was made all the easier by the fact that many were in care.

> 'There is evidence that the men deliberately targeted children who were out of control. They also targeted children who had been sent to live in care homes for precisely that reason' [153]

Those children, placed in care because their parents were not deemed good enough, were then allowed to be abused by a state that is just unable to parent. The Serious Case Review makes clear (page 10) that parents often begged agencies, including the police, to intervene and yet they did nothing. The same was true in the case of Rotherham, where the independent inquiry[154]found that an estimated 1,400 children had been abused, of which many were the subject of child protection or care orders. Page 53 of the independent inquiry's report states:

> 'It is clear that for a long period . . . some local residential units were overwhelmed by the problem of child sexual exploitation. Children who were exploited before they

[151] https://en.m.wikipedia.org/wiki/North_Wales_child_abuse_scandal, accessed 25/10/16

[152] Jay A (2014) *Independent Inquiry into Child Sexual Exploitation in Rotherham 1997-2013.* Rotherham Metropolitan Borough Council

[153] Oxfordshire Safeguarding Children Board (2015) *Serious Case Review into Child Sexual Exploitation in Oxfordshire from the Experiences of Children A, B, C, D, E and F.*

[154] Jay, A (2014) *Independent Inquiry into Child Sexual Exploitation in Rotherham 1997-2013*

became looked after continued to be exploited and they were often at even greater risk of harm. Other children became exposed to sexual exploitation for the first time whilst they were looked after in children's homes'.

At the time of writing, 2017, many more Oxford men are about to go on trial for the sexual abuse of similar children. Placing children in residential care in the UK just doesn't work, yet children repeatedly end up in such homes because foster placements are notorious for their transience. Action for Children used the Freedom of Information Act to establish that in one year, between April 2014 and March 2015,14,593 children had moved carer at least twice.[155] At 31 March 2012, only 17% of all fostered children aged between 5 and 12 had been in the same foster placement for more than five years.[156] In 2013, 41% of children were placed out of area, ie. outside of their local authority area.[157] Whilst social workers will have rationalised their decision to move the child out of area (a shortage of suitable more local foster carers/ belief that family or local community a bad influence etc), this, combined with what we know about placement breakdown, means that children lack the social cohesion that is so important to the fabric of all our lives, and that their relatives, predominantly on low incomes, cannot afford to visit them, or with other children to look after, are simply unable to do so, even if allowed.

Nor are children in care safe. In the year ending April 2016, 9% of looked after children were reported as missing. Some of these were missing only for brief

[155] Action for Children, http://www.cypnow.co.uk/cyp/news/1153856/one-in-five-foster-placements-break-down-council-data-shows, accessed 1/11/2016

[156] Department for Education (2013) *Improving permanence for looked after children.* https://www.gov.uk/government/uploads/system/uploads/attachment_data/file/264952/final_improving_permanence_data_pack_2013_sept.pdf, accessed 1/11/2016

[157] Brodie I, Dance C, Christie C, Prokop J, Cosis-Brown H (2014) *Out of borough placements for London's looked after children: A research study.* https://www.londoncouncils.gov.uk/download/file/fid/4263, *accessed 1/11/2016*

periods, such as a day, but it is cautionary to note that 50% of those reported missing were in residential homes, 35% were living with foster parents but only 1% (or only 20% of those living with their parents) were living with their parents at the time.[158] This again, sadly, links into cases such as Rotherham or Oxford, where vulnerable children were preyed on by men and went missing for periods from care.

It is reasonably common for siblings to be taken into care, but harder to find placements together for them. Sometimes professionals will find reasons to justify keeping siblings apart (a pathological cross-contamination model) yet research again and again shows that keeping siblings together is important for positive outcomes,[159] reduces the number of moves in care and child experience of loneliness, whilst leading to better outcomes in terms of behaviour and offending. Yet recent research in England by Family Rights Group, found that half of all sibling groups in local authority care had been split up.[160]

Foster placements in themselves are a flawed concept. There has always been a shortage of foster carers, and those who do step up to the plate, are under no obligation to care for the child indefinitely. If they no longer want the child, their circumstances change, or they want to move away, they can simply return the child. Further, it is estimated that per year children make 2,000 to 2,500 claims of abuse at the hands of their foster carers. Whilst only a quarter

[158] Department of Education (2016) *Children looked after in England (including adoption) year ending 31 March 2016*.https://www.gov.uk/government/uploads/system/uploads/attachment_data/file/556331/SFR41_2016_Text.pdf , *accessed 2/11/2016*

[159] See, for example, Brody et al (2008) *Placement condition, quality of the sibling relationship and child outcomes: a prospective study. USA. SAMHSA*

[160] Ashley C and Roth D (2015) *What happens to siblings in the cae system*. London. FRG http://www.frg.org.uk/images/PDFS/siblings-in-care-final-report-january-2015.pdf, accessed 2/11/2016

of these may be substantiated, it would seem unlikely that a happy child would just invent the other cases.[161] Parents, regardless whether we like them, are permanent carers. They sometimes need support, guidance even perhaps coercion, but they are just as likely as any care system to keep the child 'safe' and in the process secure the child in other ways, through keeping it within a context that is known.

In the 1960s Urie Bronfenbrenner was one of the first social psychologists to understand that interpersonal relationships, even between a parent and child, do not exist in a vacuum but are embedded in the wider ecological sphere of community, society, economics and politics. However shabby our homes, or our clothes, do they not smell of home? Can we not all remember the trauma of visiting a friend's house, of having to stay at other people's houses when young? But these children are doing it all the time; starting in new schools, eating different food, being taught different manners, different morals, and ultimately learning, if they are fortunate, to lie about their home circumstances, to make superficial friendships and to develop the anomie that is so destructive in later adult life. Little wonder that they fill the prisons, haunt the streets or die a pauper's death; or that in turn their children, fathered or mothered too early in life, go on to repeat the pattern.

Today's social workers in England use the Common Assessment Framework to assess a child's needs against five 'priority outcomes': being healthy, staying safe, enjoying and achieving, making a positive contribution and economic wellbeing. They effectively judge parenting capacity against these criteria, yet we have seen in this and other chapters that care correlates statistically with poorer health outcomes, particularly mental health, an unsafe environment, change and poor school attainment, homelessness and

---

[161] Biehal Ni, Culworth L, Wade J and Clarke S (2014) *Keeping children safe: allegations concerning the abuse or neglect of children in care.* University of York and NSPCC

offending. Both children and parents are being condemned by the very assessment used to 'help' them.

One seemingly obvious way to keep children within a known context is the use of kinship care (also called family and friends care). Such care may be a private arrangement which, if long term, may involve the relative applying for a child arrangements order and parental responsibility. On the other hand, if the child is a child protection concern, following assessment and a care order or s.20 voluntary admission to care, the child can live with a relative, friend or connected person who has been assessed and approved as a foster carer. Although the number of children in kinship care has more than doubled since 1991, the vast majority of these children (95%) are being cared for privately through the use of private law child arrangements orders, where payment is discretionary. In itself this may not be problematic, but in reality, it means that social services often do not financially support the carers, the majority of whom already live in poverty.[162] This may in turn explain why research suggests (Selwyn et al 2013)[163] that kinship care still often involves the break up of siblings. Unsupported and for the most part not paid as foster carers are, these kin carers often simply cannot manage.

Kinship care is not perfect, not least because of the lack of financial and other support. Add into this the fact that many of these children have had traumatic early lives and that Selwyn et al (2013) found that many of them had not been able to access Child and Adolescent Mental Health Services (CAMHS) or other counselling support, and we can see that these children and their kin carers are for the most part left to struggle. Countries such as Spain provide

---

[162] For these and other statistics in this section, please see:
Selwyn J, Farmer E, Meakings S and Vaisey P (2013) *The poor relations? Children and informal kin carers speak out.* University of Bristol. http://www.bristol.ac.uk/media-library/sites/sps/migrated/documents/report.pdf

[163] Selwyn et al (2013) *op cit*

an allowance for all kinship carers which enables them to bring up the child they care for and to some extent compensates the many who have had to give up their jobs to care.

Whilst there are clear benefits to properly funded kinship care, it is clear that local authorities avoid formal kinship foster care placements because of the implications for financial support. Far easier and cheaper to encourage or allow relatives to have informal private care arrangements or private law-governed arrangements (such as special guardianship or child arrangement orders). An evaluation of the work done by Family Rights Group (Ritchie 2010) records one grandparent stating -

> 'They placed the child with us, but won't admit this was not
> a private   arrangement. We needed support and there
> were contact issues, but the social workers kept fobbing us
> off . . . Not doing their job. The child was referred to
> CAMHS but it took years to get help. We also had financial
> problems. We were up to our eyes in debt at the time, but
> our income looked good on paper. We couldn't get legal
> aid'.[164]

Where children are already on care orders, the choice of kinship care is also frequently disregarded. The most frequent reason given may be that of a cross-contamination model, or a fear that the grandparent or relative is too old or too disabled to cope despite their protestations. Family Rights Group has rightly argued that Government guidance should direct local authorities to try first to place looked after children with willing kinship/family and

---

[164] Ritchie C (2010) *Evaluation of Family Rights Group's advice service.* London: Family Rights Group
https://www.frg.org.uk/images/PDFS/advice-service-evaluation-executive-summary-2010.pdf

friends carers provided that so doing would be consistent with the child's welfare.[165] One way of approaching this, is through the use of Family Group Conferences, which is addressed in more detail in chapter five. There is also a case for saying that given the uncertainties around legal aid for private law applications, the law should enable parental responsibility to be obtained by allowing parents to enter into a parental responsibility agreement with a relative, as happens already with step parents.

Prioritising kinship/family and friend care over and above unrelated foster care, institutional care or adoption offers a way forward. At present, often surprised and uninformed family members, frequently grandparents, find themselves struggling with low incomes, a complicated legal system and a new child to support whilst children's services appear to have an erratic and unstructured approach to kinship care that can penalise kin carers who apply to be formal foster carers, and therefore receive foster carer rates of pay, by failing them at assessment.

Unless we reduce radically the number of children in care, and promote kinship care where care is needed, we shall continue the broken system that currently punishes those who have no power and little voice. The author today, in 2017, worked as she does every week in a local advice centre. In came a 25 year old EU national with her nine month old child and an outreach worker. They had come for help with an eviction notice given by the local authority. The woman, who had worked for several years in the UK before giving birth, had found her child - possibly as a result of a violent ex partner - the subject of a care order. The child had been fostered, but as the mother had no difficulties with parenting, the child had been returned to her following a case conference involving her social worker and other

[165] Aziz R, Roth D, Lindley B and Ashley C (2012) *Understanding family and friends care: The largest UK survey. London:* Family Rights Group
http://www.frg.org.uk/images/e-publications/ffc-summary-3.pdf

professionals, including housing. She had been recently placed in a local authority flat, the rent for which exceeded £800 a month. Because of her relatively recent immigration status and her failure to work since having the baby, she is not entitled to any benefits except, for the child, child benefit. So the housing authority had offered her accommodation, knowing that she had no means of paying for it, no access to housing benefit or council tax reduction, and no family here to help her with child care. As an unskilled worker with no family in England, she has no way of earning enough to pay even the rent, let alone utilities and child care whilst she works. We are fighting for her, but her social worker is new and doesn't answer her phone, and her outreach worker is also new and knows nothing of the case. The easiest option will be for the social worker to press the case for the welfare of the child, take the child into foster care, possibly seeking an adoption order, and leave the mother to fend for herself on the streets. Perhaps by the time I have finished this book, she will be there.

Earlier in the week I had visited another mother, an ex heroin addict in hospital. She is about to be discharged back onto the streets, as she has been homeless since her six week old baby was taken into care. As she says, when her daughter was taken from her, even though she was then in accommodation, she 'just lost it'. She has her daughter's photo in her wallet. She received a letter informing her that her daughter had now been formally adopted and this had precipitated an overdose.

It is time to break the cycle, to learn from other countries, and to develop a social care system for families that really works.

KEY POINTS

1) Frontline care home staff, including managers, are under qualified and lack professional standing.

2) Experience of being in care is correlated with early pregnancy, frequent moves within care, high risk of out-of-area placement, the break-up of siblings groups and poor outcomes in education, mental health, offending behaviour, homelessness and life chances.

3) The prevalence of abuse in care and the poor outcomes for care leavers are evidence that the state is unable to parent.

4) There is no evidence that care saves lives and plenty of evidence that an experience of care is linked with poor outcomes.

5) Prioritising the use of family group conferences and kinship/family and friends care can offer a way forward if it is properly supported.

QUESTIONS FOR DISCUSSION

1) Given that most incidences of care home abuse has been attributed to men, how can children best be protected?

2) Is there any justification for the current system of stranger foster care or care homes?

3) Should parents always have a right to visit and see their child on a reasonably regular basis, even if supervised, unless convicted of a serious offence against them? What are the risks and benefits?

CHAPTER FOUR
A PUBLIC HEALTH APPROACH

Why Are Poor Parents More Vulnerable?

So far we have seen that time and again it is the poorest whose children are taken into care whilst their wealthier counterparts rarely come under the spotlight. The classic study by Bebbington and Miles (1989)[166] looked at the odds for coming into care.

CHILD A	CHILD B
•Age 5 - 9	•Child B
•No supplemental benefit	•Age 5 – 9
•2 parent family	•Supplemental benefit
•Three or fewer children	•Single adult household
•White	
•Owner occupier house	
•More rooms than people	
•Odds of entering care are 1 in 7,000	Odds of entering care are 1 in 10

Yet the evidence for more 'abusive' parenting amongst any one social class is scant. A study by Ritchie and Buchanan (2009)[167], using a sample of 391 young people aged 13 to 15, found that parenting was similar cross-class but that pupils from private schools reported a greater incidence of negative parenting in 11 categories: Mum or Dad not interested in me, Mum or Dad

---

[166] Bebbington A and Miles J (1989) The background of children who enter local authority care. *British Journal of Social Work*. 19 (1): 349-368.

[167] Ritchie, C and Buchanan, A. (2009) Self report of parenting style, socio-economic status and psychological functioning in a sample of 13-15 year old students. *Journal of Social Work*, July 2010 10: 317-332.

frightening me, Mum or Dad being often angry with me, Mum or Dad treating me unkindly, Dad not being loving, Mum or Dad sometimes hitting me quite hard, and Mum or Dad sometimes hitting partner. In six of those categories the difference in the proportion of private school pupils reporting the negative parenting style in question was stastically significant (<5%): Dad not interested in me (12.5% of private school pupils v. 5% of special measures[168] school pupils), Dad sometimes frightens me (33.8% of private school pupils v. 16.7% of special measures school pupils), Mum sometimes frightens me (16.9% of private school pupils v. 10% special measures school pupils), Dad treats me unkindly (9.2% of private school pupils v. 1.7% of special measures school children), Dad not loving (16.9% of private school pupils v. 11.7% of special measures school children), and Dad sometimes hitting hard (10.8% of private school pupils v. 5% of special measures school children).

Negative parenting styles also tended to correlate with higher student scores on the Strengths and Difficulties Questionnaire, suggesting increased risk for psychological disturbance/stress.

Many of those entering care come from families where a parent themselves was in care. Such families are already under a spotlight, and as we have seen in chapter 2, an experience of care tends towards increased risk of making a poor marriage, mental health problems, homelessness and so on. But for the others entering care, vulnerability is linked overwhelmingly to poverty and unequal access to opportunity and support. Add to this that precipitous stressors such as violence, alcohol abuse, and psychotic episodes are, for the poor, often triggered by the situation in which they find themselves. Those reading this book have agency; they feel able to act in most spheres of their lives. Those on low incomes often feel powerless; in debt, no security of tenure, with more physical and mental health problems, with more children to provide for and with less opportunity to do so.

---

[168] Special measures being defined as a school found by Ofsted inspectors to be falling below the required standard.

Life Event	Options for Social Class: A, B, C1	Options for Social Class C2, D, E
Violent Partner who refuses to leave	Seek legal action for criminal proceedings, injunction, Occupation Order, and/or divorce. Financial capacity to rent/ purchase as last resort. Less likely to be homeless, less likely to have to choose between him and homelessness/a refuge.	May get legal aid but requires evidence. May get help if council owned. Can apply to County Court under PartIV Schedule 7 of the Family Law Act 1996 and get tenancy agreement transferred to victim's name but not available to most private rented sector tenants on assured shorthold tenancies. Police can use Domestic Violence Protection Notices/ apply for Orders to exclude perpetrator. Victim likely to have to choose between him and homelessness/temporary B&B accommodation or a refuge.

Life Event	Options for Social Class: A, B, C1	Options for Social Class C2, D, E
Over use of alcohol or drugs (physical, emotional abuse; neglect. Risk)	Tend to drink at home, behind doors. Seen as socially acceptable, but still link with violence. Use of drugs similar cross class but middle and upper classes have fewer risk factors for problematic/ addicted behaviours, are more aspirational and likely to be in good education or employment.	Tend to drink in pubs or street, not socially acceptable, link with violence. Particular subgroups at greater risk of problematic drug use, eg. homeless, ex-care, excluded from school, offending behaviour, mental health issues. Care leavers prominent. Thought that for these subgroups persistent use may be rational choice, ie. to numb pain of lives/blot out lack of hope (Neale 2002; Edwards 2004. Rowntree 1901)

Life Event	Options for Social Class: A, B, C1	Options for Social Class C2, D, E
Serious and enduring mental health issues (emotional abuse/neglect/ risk)	Mental health problems less prevalent in better off. Better off are better served by GPs (Hart 1971) Can afford counselling Use of au pairs, nannies, alternative private day care or boarding schools	Poverty linked to increase in mental heath problems but poorer access to services. Long waits for counselling and shortage of psychiatric beds. No money for child care, nannies, au pairs, boarding schools etc. Constant level of stressors linked with poverty, eg. debt, risk of homelessness, disability.
Single parent with young children who needs medical or other time out.	More likely to be home owner with income sufficient to meet bills and pay for additional child care.	Less likely to be home owner, more likely to lead to rent arrears and further debt. No spare cash for additional child care.

Life Event	Options for Social Class: A, B, C1	Options for Social Class C2, D, E
Unable to bond with child; emotionally detached (emotional abuse)	More likely to be aware of risk of post natal depression, more likely to belong to support groups such as the Natural Childbirth Trust. Can afford alternative care providers, nannies, child care, boarding schools.	Less likely to be aware of post natal depression, less likely to have access to alternative child care provision. More likely to be socially isolated and poor. Many of the poorest will be single women with children, barely able to keep body and soul together.

Life Event	Options for Social Class: A, B, C1	Options for Social Class C2, D, E
Parent brought up in care	Unlikely. No-one is really looking at these children or their parents.	By definition a less than easy childhood. Little experience of parenting or of having needs met. Little experience of how to maintain a family: banking, accessing services, managing budgets, etc. No role models Experience of care often chaotic, sometimes abusive. Linked with early parenthood, to unstable fathers, higher risk of substance misuse and mental health problems. Known to social services and therefore vulnerable to care proceedings for own children.

Life Event	Options for Social Class: A, B, C1	Options for Social Class C2, D, E
Has problems with anger management (physical and emotional abuse)	Unlikely to be on social services' radar, able to afford nannies/au pairs/ private schooling with longer hours. Research (Ritchie 2004) suggests these problems may be more prevalent in wealthier families.	Children more likely to be on radar of social services, other stressors more likely to lead to increased stress/ risk of anger. No money for extra help with child care.
Sexually abused as a child	Unlikely to come to the attention of social services.	More likely to come to attention of social services, especially if parent has experience of care/was sexually abused in care or in family home.
Single parent on benefits	Statistically less likely to be in this social group.	Being a single parent linked with poverty, risk of debt, rent arrears and additional stressors.

Life Event	Options for Social Class: A, B, C1	Options for Social Class C2, D, E
No time or inclination to spend time with child (neglect)	Can arrange for child care and private schooling to fill the child's days and to an extent these can act as protective factors for child.	Child is literally neglected as no social structures in place to compensate for lack of stimulation and affection.

Life Event	Options for Social Class: A, B, C1	Options for Social Class C2, D, E
Partner in prison or long-term hospitalisation	Less likely in these social groups. Can move if social stigma attaches. Has income/skills to work/ recourse to boarding schools. Moves to interest only mortgage	More likely in these social groups. Remaining parent under increased stress, financial hardship. Partner often far away as shortage of psychiatric beds and prison places locally. Mothers in prison for prostitution/drug offending at risk of suicide. It is estimated that more than 17,240 children were separated from their mothers in 2010 by imprisonment. Only 9% of children whose mothers are in prison are cared for by their fathers in their mothers' absence. At least a fifth of women prisoners are lone parents

* Refs: [169], [170], *

Taking each issue in turn - a public health approach

Domestic Violence

We know the effect that violence, including coercion, manipulation and marital rape, can have on children. Some children end up in care because the victim (usually the mother), cannot provide a home or place of safety. It is interesting to note that in 2017, Citizens Advice, a respected source of support in England and Wales States on their website that -

'If you are a victim of an abusive relationship you may need somewhere safe to stay, either alone or with your children. The options are:

- stay at home if you think this is safe
- stay with relatives or friends
- stay in a women's refuge. This is only an option for women (with or without children)
- get emergency accommodation from the local authority under homeless persons law - this will usually mean a bed and breakfast hostel
- get privately rented accommodation.,[171]

For mothers, home is key; not 'home if you think it's safe'. Whilst violence in the home is frequently difficult to prosecute due to lack of independent witnesses or victim reluctance to expose herself to further risk, it cannot be

---

[169] Social class is approximated using NRS classifications.

[170] Neale J (2002) Drug users in society. Basingstoke: Palgrave
Edwards G (2004) Matters of substance - drugs and why everyone's a user. London: Penguin Books
5. http://www.poverty.org.uk/07/index.shtml?7, accessed 23/11/2016

[171] Citizens Advice https://www.citizensadvice.org.uk/relationships/gender-violence/domestic-violence-and-abuse/#h-options-available-to-people-affected-by-domestic-violence

acceptable that the presumption should always favour the perpetrator so that it is the mother and children who must protect themselves by flight.

Let us assume that Anna lives with partner Shane in private rented accommodation. Shane has knocked Anna about several times when he's drunk. He's always sorry afterwards but last time their son saw it all. Anna asked him to leave. He refused, they argued and he dragged her by her hair into the kitchen, picked up a knife, then threw it down and stormed out of the door. Their son saw this too. She rang the police. As she had no witness other than her three year old son, no obvious signs of bruising, and her partner denied it, they felt there was not enough evidence to take the matter further or issue a Domestic Violence Protection Notice. They suggested she contact a solicitor and apply under civil law (which requires a lower threshold of proof than criminal law) for a Domestic Violence Protection Order and/or an Occupation Order (excluding him from the property). They explained that the Order could protect her from further abuse, and ban him from returning to the home and contacting her. If the perpetrator did not keep to the Order, he could be arrested and brought before the court.

Anna was afraid to stay even one more day in that house. She went to a solicitor but was told that although she might qualify for legal aid, she would need evidence or at the very least a letter from her GP or social services. She saw her GP who suggested child protection social workers might help. The social worker carried out an assessment of Anna and parenting capacity but she did not meet Shane. She warned Anna that if she could not go to the police or provide evidence, she would have to consider a refuge. The nearest one was twenty miles away - far from everything she knew and she had no income of her own. As Anna prevaricated the violence escalated until one of her neighbours reported her screams to the police. The police arrested Shane and her son was taken into care under an Emergency Protection Order.

The tenancy agreement was in Shane's name, and Anna cannot afford the rent anyway on her own. She has moved into a women's refuge in that distant town. Her son has been returned to her but social workers are considering whether to make a care order, as Anna is now suffering from depression and anxiety. After six months, Anna is moved into hostel bed and breakfast accommodation with her son, who is now on a care order for emotional abuse. Anna is borderline hospitalisation, can no longer adequately interact with her son, and spends much of her day rocking to and fro in the small bedroom which she shares with him. The case conference decided that he should have a place at a local nursery, but there is no accommodation for them in the foreseeable future. Shane, however, who received a police caution, still lives at his old address with a new partner, who is expecting their first child in January.

Although a woman can now apply in person at a police station, under 'Clare's Law', to find out whether her partner has a record of domestic violence, uptake has been slow and part of any abuser's approach is to groom the victim so that they come to trust and rely on them. Once women realise that they are in physical or mental danger, they need to be able to act quickly, not by being forced out of the family home, but by being able to obtain, within 24 hours of application, an Occupation Order granted even where the evidence may as yet be unreliable. Applications can be done in this way now, but ex parte applications are not the norm. There is an argument that ex parte, even with very little 'evidence', can be the norm. In these circumstances someone is going to suffer; but it is far preferable for the parent and child to stay in the home, safe and secure, and to risk a miscarriage of justice for the accused than for the accused to get the home with the parent and child forced onto the caprices of the welfare state or the charitable sector.

Overuse of Alcohol or Drugs

We've seen that particular subgroups - the homeless, those with a history of offending and school exclusion, and those with mental health problems - are at particular risk for problematic drug and alcohol abuse. We also know that a high proportion of them will be ex care leavers. Young people in care aged 11 to 19, for example, have a fourfold increased risk of drug and alcohol use, and a fivefold increased risk of developing at least one mental health disorder, compared with those not in care, and a national survey found that 32% of care leavers smoked marijuana daily. This is the highly visible group: the poor and vulnerable who cope with their lives through drinking and taking drugs, often in public places. They come easily under the eye of social workers, and are often known to social workers from a young age. When their substance misuse gets too bad, their children go into care. Just as, in 2017, our prisons are full of ex care leavers, so are our streets. There is only one solution; to break the cycle.

For addicts, whatever the addiction, the aim must be to create a safe, warm and nurturing environment. A wealthy addict, such as Keith Richards, can afford au pairs and nannies and an easy supply of drugs or alcohol, a poor addict has neither support nor supply, leading to often chaotic lifestyles where caring for anyone is even more difficult amidst the frequently associated problems of debt, risk of eviction and offending. The seemingly easy Dr Barnardo solution is to take the child out of the home. But we know that in the long term, the child is frequently damaged by care. The more challenging option is to set up more parent and child rehab residential clinics in England and Wales, and to train the social and/or pedagogic work force so that parents feel encouraged and supported in going with their children into rehab. Projects, which are few and far between currently, such as the Trevi Project in Plymouth,[172]can offer residential and ongoing support, thus obviating the

---

[172] http://www.treviproject.org/testimonials

more costly and damaging (in both the present and for future generations) option of taking the children into care. Yet still today, in my own experience, I have found that poorly trained and resourced social workers and housing officers are far too quick to take the simple course of action - evict the mother for dealing/rent arrears and take the children into care - than to build for the future. It takes training, it takes resources (although fewer), it takes belief that the poor, like the rich, can be redeemed, and it takes clear policy and professional direction.

Old/Current Cycle: In use since mid 19th Century

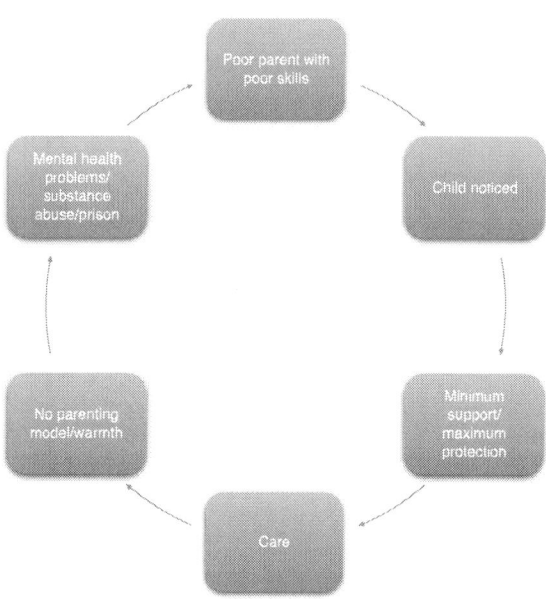

Cost analysis of Old/Current Cycle

Poor parent with poor skills > no early years exposure to better modelling > minimal financial provision for support > child protection concerns > costly child protection interventions/care order applications/conferences > care (£29,000-£33,000pa per foster placement and £131,000-£135,000 pa per child on residential placements)[173] > mental health/homeless/substance abuse support > poor parenting > Minimal financial provision for support, and round it goes.

Proposed Model In use from 2020

Poor parent with poor skills > public health nationwide campaign on how to 'parent' > Family Nurse Partnership rolled out nationwide >from age 2, equivalent of free French Ecole Maternelle, with *optional* attendance > all schools/early years to adopt whole school approach > persistent child difficulty > support, if necessary in-home additional support > trained pedagogic work force > aim and outcome, fewer than 10,000 in care (currently 80,000+) > next generation of better parents.

Post natal depression and/or psychosis

The key to obtaining support for post natal depression or psychosis is early recognition and positive support. If the Family Nurse Partnership became universal, rather than targeted merely at identified vulnerable families, it is likely that mental health issues would be quickly identified. Leaving new mothers to get on with it very quickly after a birth, and making that the norm - rather than, as in the old days or within some cultures in the UK, making the birth a time of NHS support through available beds and visiting midwives - leaves many new mothers isolated, especially where they are lone parents. The point is not that they are ill and need treatment, but that well people who have been through the massive shock and change of child birth need support,

---

[173] National Audit Office (2015) Children in Care: Report by the Comptroller & Auditor General: Department of Education. HC 737. Session 2014-2015

warmth and guidance from a positive perspective. If that is missing, not only does that undermine one of the most important investments in our lifetimes, but it also means that symptoms of post-natal depression (PND) or psychosis may not be noticed.

Whether or not a woman is suffering from depression or PND, not all women immediately love their children. Some will always find it difficult to want to be close with their child. We need to create a nurturing society in which mothers, in particular, but also fathers can feel safe to express how they feel, so that with the support of others they can find a way of living with the new family that suits them. Feeling inadequate, angry, overtired or irritated by the newborn are all within the spectrum of parenting and parents, all parents, need to be able to discuss their feelings without fear of judgement. The role of FNPs in particular is vital in creating a trusting bond between professional and parent. One which enables all difficulties to be discussed and resolved and that also allows early signs of mental health issues to be identified and treated. It is surely not good enough for family nurse partnerships to be available only to those deemed vulnerable. In that way many will be missed and others feel stigmatised. In providing state care through the NHS we have lost some of the things that came naturally in earlier societies, and one of those is the importance of knowing where positive support lies within the community. When I was young, Fanny the post woman was also the person who laid people out upon death. Now those vital transitions of birth, marriage and death are left to the state or to business. A universal Family Nurse Partnership programme, available to all and invested in by the state can offer real support through a child's first two years, and avoid the hospitalisation, neglect, or need for care that are so costly both to the public purse and, more importantly, to people's lives.

A Public Health Approach to Mental Health

We know that mental health problems are linked to risk for emotional abuse or neglect, or in extremis, to child injury/death. We also know that the vast majority of those with mental health problems are excellent parents. So why are proportionally more children in care from amongst the poor?

One factor is that the prevalence of mental health problems is greater amongst women than men, more single parents are women and we know that being a single parent is linked to poverty. Mental health issues such as clinical depression, schizophrenia, and psychosis are also linked to an accumulation

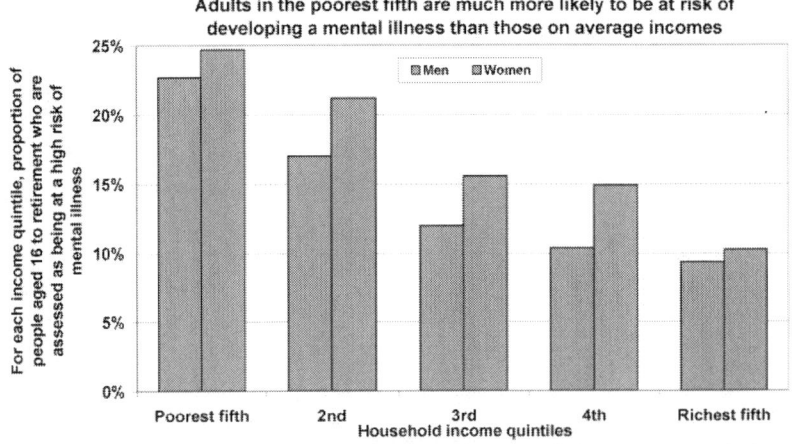

Adults in the poorest fifth are much more likely to be at risk of developing a mental illness than those on average incomes

Source: Health Survey for England, DH; the data is the average for 2008 and 2009; England; updated Mar 2011

of stressors, which in turn is a phenomenon linked disproportionately to low income thus indicating a causal relationship with poverty as the driver (Hudson 2005)[174]. Although many of us may have a genetic predisposition towards mental illness, for the most part it is less likely to be triggered by stressful life events.

---

[174] Hudson, C.G., "Socioeconomic Status and Mental Illness: Tests of the Social Causation and Selection Hypotheses," American Journal of Orthopsychiatry, Vol. 75, No. 1, pp. 3-18, 2005

From a public health and primary prevention perspective the medical model is largely unhelpful. Whilst pharmacological solutions may damp down symptoms, they will not prevent onset. The key here is to address the harder task of reducing accumulations of life stressors, which in turn means addressing the social determinants of health; reducing poverty, unemployment, low educational/skill attainment and inequality, and increasing home 'ownership'/security and job security. A strategic consideration might also be a long-overlooked recognition of parenting as work. Where one parent chooses or needs to stay at home with a child/children who is/are under the age of five, it should be encouraged not only by payment, but also be ensuring affordable child care is also accessible. In England, for example, such a parent might be entitled to housing and council tax benefit and income support, but her (use of 'her' to include 'his') income will be extremely low, placing her below the poverty line. The same is true of working families, where the Institute of Fiscal Studies found that the proportion of children in poverty living in a working families rose from 54% in 2009–10 to 63% by 2013–14.[175]

A welfare state condoned culture of refusing to recognise the care of under fives as work hits the most vulnerable the hardest. Forced to survive on income support or very low partner wages, they are the ignored underbelly of England. Whilst disability rights campaigners and charities such as Age Concern rightly fight for Carers Allowance and Attendance Allowance to increase, at least it is recognised that the elderly and disabled need care. It is not recognised nearly enough, but it is established. The care of children, however, our future, our hopes and our dreams, is deemed worthless by the state. True that there is some free provision for 3 and 4 year olds but this is

---

[175] Institute of Fiscal Studies (2015) Living Standards, Poverty and Inequality in the UK: 2015. London: Joseph Rowntree Foundation

too little too late for children who are already educationally disadvantaged, and to help parents struggling with younger children and babies as well as with the blight of debt and poverty.

A parent, and particularly a lone parent, suffering from a severe mental illness will often seek help, whilst also mindful that her children are her first priority. A lone mother may be desperate for help, but will balk at persuading her GP to admit her, let alone acknowledge her slipping grasp on reality, for fear that the children may be taken away. There is no-one waiting to step into the breach; no-one saying, 'Come to me and I will give you rest', there are only drugs, the long wait for admission to a psychiatric hospital, and the knowledge that your children are unlikely to be supported in their own homes. This situation is not only far less prevalent among the better off, but also much easier to resolve. Where a parent needs respite, admission to a psychiatric hospital or just 'time out', there is money with which to pay for child care, a nanny or even private counselling. The poor can afford none of these.

Perinatal mental health problems can be supported and addressed through public health initiatives such as the Family Nurse Partnership but lack of funding means that it is accessible only to the few. Mother and baby mental health units can also offer support and respite, but again they are few and far between. Given that a systematic review suggests their efficacy (Willham and Wittkowski 2015),[176] there are in reality very few within England and Wales, and in the whole of the UK there are only 17 specialist community perinatal mental health teams (current provision as at 2016).[177] This means that for

[176] Gillham R and Wittkowski A (2015)Outcomes for women admitted to a mother and baby unit: a systematic review. *International Journal of Women's Health.* 7: 459-476. https:// www.ncbi.nlm.nih.gov/pmc/articles/PMC4425328/#

[177] http://everyonesbusiness.org.uk/?page_id=349, accessed 28/11/2016

most lone parents, without other support, the options are bleak, especially where there are other young children in the home. It is not good enough that they should have to rely on the facilities offered, or not, by local charities. We would not tolerate this for incapacitating physical illness.

One solution is for local authorities to commission/provide a nannying service available to those on low incomes to support them, in the parental home if necessary, through times of crisis. Sounds crazy? Just think of the army of carers serving older people; it's in the same mould but would only be needed where there is a perceived risk to child AND parent. In this way children can remain in their own homes, amongst their familiar things, attending their usual school and as little disturbed as possible. Such a service should always be available where a parent has experienced severe psychosis/ depression and returned home after hospitalisation. We know from research that this is a period where young children and the parent themselves may be at greatest risk and it is not good enough to provide intermittent support even if, for example with the Care Programme Approach, it is daily.

Further, any parent suffering from a severe form of mental illness should be asked about filicidal ideation, in the same way as we now accept that we should ask about suicidal ideation. Just as there is no evidence to suggest that such a move increases the incidence of suicide, so in filicide it would not increase risk to the child but rather give the parent an opportunity to explore their ideas. Many of those who have killed their children have done so for altruistic reasons, believing them to be better off in heaven than with their father or for delusional reasons such as that they are 'evil'. These mental states are treatable but only if they are first addressed (see, for example, Friedman and Resnick 2007).[178] Living in fear that your children may be

---

[178] Friedman S and Resnick P (2007) Child murder by mothers: patterns and prevention. *Journal of World Psychiatry, 6,* 137-141. https://www.ncbi.nlm.nih.gov/pmc/articles/PMC2174580/#, accessed 30/11/2016

taken from you if the powers that be know how you think is unhelpful and dangerous. Living in the knowledge that you will be supported and treated and that your children will not have to leave either your or your home offers hope, safety and familiar context for both parent and child.

Parents in prison

In 1980, Chris Tchaikovsky, herself once in prison, set up a UK based charity, Women in Prison. Her view was clearly stated -

"Taking the most hurt people out of society and punishing them in order to teach them how to live within society is, at best, futile. Whatever else a prisoner knows, she knows everything there is to know about punishment because that is exactly what she has grown up with. Whether it is childhood sexual abuse, indifference, neglect; punishment is most familiar to her."

Yet in the past few years the number of women in prison, many of them parents, has increased substantially.

<u>Who are the women in prison?</u>[179]

- 46% of women in prison report have suffered domestic violence
- 53% of women in prison report having experienced emotional, physical or sexual abuse during childhood.
- 31% women in prison have spent time in local authority care as a child.

<u>What have they done?</u>

- 81% of women are serving a prison sentence for a non-violent crime.
- 26% of all women in prison had no previous convictions, compared to 12% of men.
- Theft and handling was by far the most common offence, accounting for 40% of all sentenced women in the year 2013.

---

[179] http://www.womeninprison.org.uk/research/key-facts.php

- Women in custody are five times more likely to have a mental health concern than women in the general population.
- Of all the women who are sent to prison, 46% say they have attempted suicide at some time in their life.
- There have been 100 deaths of women in prison since 200, and in 2016 alone, the latest year for which figures are available, 19 women prisoners had taken their own lives.[180]

Women prisoners, drugs and alcohol

- In 2010, 24% of women in prison were serving sentences for drug offences.
- 48% of women have committed their offence in order to support the drug use of someone else.
- 52% of women surveyed said that they had used heroin, crack, or cocaine in the four weeks prior to custody. However, practitioners report that women may hide or underplay substance misuse through fear of losing their children.

How do we look after the family?

- More than 17,240 children were separated from their mothers in 2010 by imprisonment.
- Only 9% of children whose mothers are in prison are cared for by their fathers in their mothers' absence.
- No-one routinely monitors the parental status of prisoners in the UK or systematically identifies children of prisoners, where they live or which

[180] The Guardian, 29 October 2016, https://www.theguardian.com/society/2016/oct/29/prison-suicides-record-levels-scandal

services they are accessing. Where this information is collected, it is patchy and not always shared.[181]

- According to 2005 research from Alison Liebling, two-thirds of imprisoned women are mothers of children under 18. A third of these have children under five, and a further 40 per cent have children between five and ten.[182]

- Only half of the women who had lived with or were in contact with their children prior to imprisonment had received a visit since going to prison, with many mothers hundreds of miles from their low-income families and the average distance from home being 60 miles.

- One Home Office study showed that for 85% of mothers, prison was the first time they had been separated from their children for any significant length of time .

- Imprisoning mothers for non-violent offences has a damaging impact on children and carries a cost to the state of more than £17 million over a ten year period.

On release

- Around one-third of women prisoners lose their homes, and often their possessions, while in prison.[183]

- A Prisons Inspectorate survey found that 38% of women in prison did not have accommodation arranged on release.

Frequently homeless, their children in care, it is unsurprising that in 2010, 45% of women leaving prison were reconvicted within one year. With children lost to care, homeless and with none to love them save the bad company they

---

[181] Bromley Briefings Prison Factfile, Autumn 2016, at http://www.prisonreformtrust.org.uk/Portals/0/Documents/Bromley%20Briefings/Autumn%202016%20Factfile.pdf

[182] http://www.womensbreakout.org.uk/about-us/key-facts/

[183]Wedderburn, D. (2000) Justice for Women: The Need for Reform, London: Prison Reform Trust)

now know, the reoffenders then for the most part continue inexorably in and out of prison with more children appearing and then disappearing within the 'care' of the state.[184]

Community Solutions

Women in Prison, founded by the late Chris Tchaikovsky, report that in 2011 a higher proportion of women than men completed their community sentence successfully or had their sentences terminated for good progress on both community orders (70%) and suspended sentence orders (76%) versus 65 and 67% respectively for men. In other words, except where prison is for the safety of others, there is no reason to lock up women. If they are imprisoned, the evidence suggests family breakdown, recidivism and a lifetime in and out of prison with children all in care. If they are given community orders, especially if accompanied by training and parenting courses, and where appropriate, drug rehabilitation, many of these women could go on to live fulfilling lives with their children.

The biggest single stumbling block is likely to be drug or alcohol use and dependence on criminal men. Again, Women in Prison report that -
- In 2010, 24% of women in prison were serving sentences for drug offences.
- 48% of women committed their offence in order to support the drug use of someone else.
- 59% of women in prison who drank in the four weeks before custody thought they had a problem with alcohol.
- 52% of women surveyed said that they had used heroin, crack, or cocaine in the four weeks prior to custody. However, practitioners report that women may hide or underplay substance misuse through fear of losing their children.[185]

---

[184] http://www.womeninprison.org.uk/research/key-facts.php

[185] http://www.womeninprison.org.uk/research/key-facts.php

Unless these issues are addressed, the vicious cycle will continue, not only of recidivism and homelessness, but also of children going into care in preparation for their own lives in and out of drugs, subject often to controlling men and prison. In the USA, Drug Courts have seemingly had some success in addressing addictions and reducing recidivism but arguably at the price of denying defendants the right to pursue their case.[186] In the UK, the answer may be not to copy but to build on the American model, putting public health, women and families first and dogma last.

When women are in prison, it is crucial that proper arrangements should be made at sentencing, for contact with children (where appropriate) and the future. It is simply not good enough for judges to pass sentence with no idea of where that mother is going, or how her frequently impoverished family are to see her. Nor is it acceptable that a third of women should lose their homes whilst in prison. It is simple for the state to put the children into care, and to let the council or private landlord evict the tenant for non-payment of rent, but this is the situation that all too frequently arises when simplistic legislation, which puts the welfare of the child as the paramount consideration - however well meaning - is followed. That home was the children's home, linked to school and context. If the mother cannot be there for a short sentence of imprisonment, steps should be taken to ensure that the children remain in the home - if no relatives are available - and that the rent is suspended until release. Keeping children in the home is not rocket science; it's what the wealthy do all the time through the use of qualified nannies and proper supervision.

If the mother faces a long prison sentence and the home, and with it the children, cannot be maintained, steps should be taken to ensure that mothers

[186]https://www.nij.gov/topics/courts/drug-courts/Pages/work.aspx

are not only ready to be released through rehabilitation, parenting classes and job training, but also that accommodation is available to them on release that is suitable for a family. A mother cannot hope to regain her children from care if she is housed in a room or temporary bed and breakfast accommodation. It is just another slap in the face and another invitation to reoffend.

Single/lone parents on benefits

Single parenthood can be a sign of strength, independence or circumstance, such as divorce or widowhood. But it can also be a sign that a parent finds it difficult to form lasting relationships. Either way, a semi or non-skilled single parent of a pre-school child may have to live on benefits because their working income from a part-time, or even full-time job would not be sufficient to pay for additional child care, and as we have seen, parenting is not seen as something meritorious of pay in itself. Thus children of single parents are twice as likely to live in relative poverty as those in couple families (44 per cent and 24 per cent respectively).[187]

This group is therefore more vulnerable to their children going into care because they lack the resources to pay for support when things become difficult and because they lack a significant other and frequently, wider family, who can provide support at key times. Where single parents, for example, need psychiatric hospitalisation or care, help with addictions, help with an abusive relationship or just emotional support, there is frequently no-one there to provide for them and their children.

Of course all of these children have fathers, but frequently maintenance and contact are missing from the lives of those mothers with the most problems.

[187] Department of Work and Pensions (2016) Households below average income. 1994-95 2014-2015.

Research by Blazey and Persson (2010)[188] into how to better support parents who were the subject of care proceedings, found that the social workers made no reference to fathers in just under half of the care proceeding cases studied, whilst in the remaining cases, the number of fathers was twice the number of mothers, ie. single mothers often have children with different fathers. Although it is possible to make these situations work to the benefit of all, it is no doubt harder. For example, one study found that 64% of lone parents on benefit received no maintenance, and that the average payment to those who did, was £23 a week.[189]

Lone parenting can therefore be more problematic because of the link with poverty and lack of support. Where these two combine, the effect can be toxic. Thus unemployed or low income lone parents are more likely to suffer from poor physical and mental health than couple parents.[190] Similarly, their children are more likely to have poorer cognitive and behavioural outcomes by age 5, and to have poorer physical and mental health at age 7 than couple parents or lone parents not in poverty.[191]

Public health approaches

We have already seen that one policy approach might be to ensure that all adults have bank accounts in their own, and not joint, names. Further, fathers

---

[188] Blazey E and Persson E (2010) What can professionals do to support mothers whose previous children have been removed: an exploratory study. London: CWDC

[189] Bryson et al (2012)Survey of relationship breakdown.

[190] Burstrom et al (2010) *General Household Survey; Marryat L and Martin C* (2010) *Growing up in Scotland: maternal health and its impact on child behaviour and development.* The Scottish Government. Cooper et al (2008) *British National Psychiatric Morbidity Survey.*

[191] Milennium Cohort Study (Kiernan and Mensah 2009; Schoon L, Jones E, Cheng H and Maughan B (2012) Family hardship, family instability and cognitive development. *Journal of Epidemiology and Community Health.* 66(8): 716-22. Pearce A, Lewis H and Law C (2013) *The role of poverty in explaining health variations in 7 year old children from different family structures: findings from the UK Millennium Cohort Study. Journal of Epidemiology and Community Health* 67(2): 181-189.

(or, where applicable, mothers) of any children should have a universalised percentage docked from their pay, via PAYE, and transferred to the main carer.

Another option, might be to pay mothers, or whoever is the main carer, on a sliding scale salary that accounts for number of children under 5, child disability, and so on which is only forfeited when the main carer earns above a certain threshold. Forbes, for example, has estimated that a woman working in the home, based on the amount and type of work done in a sample of over 6,000 women at home with young children, found that their pay should be valued at about US $115,000 pa.[192] Over the years there have been feminist and other arguments for and against paying women for their work in the home, with some feminists arguing that this would reinforce stereotypes and act as a golden handcuff to the home. In today's environment, when men can also be the main carer, that argument becomes weaker. Add to this the realisation that women now feel both economically and socially forced to work in order to survive in a post-liberal world, and it is not hard to see that one way for women and men to assert their worth, in a career that is arguably more important than any for our futures, is to campaign for a main carer wage.

In Finland, since 1990, all parents of children up to the age of three have been allowed a choice between home-care payments or a place for their child in a crèche/daycare centre.

One parent could also take unpaid employment leave until the child's third birthday. For those who decide to stay at home with their young children under school age (six), the child home-care allowance is tax deductible, and

[192] https://www.forbes.com/sites/jennagoudreau/2011/05/02/why-stay-at-home-moms-should-earn-a-115000-salary/#2c6d4b2375f4, accessed 27/1/2017

available to all families with children under 3, who are not in municipal day care and for other children of the same family who are under school age. It is paid to the nominated main carer who could also be, for example, a grandparent. It includes a basic care allowance and families may also be entitled to care supplements, depending on their size and income. The allowance is linked to Finland's National Pensions Index. Just over a third (38% of families took up the home-care allowance for children aged under 2 and under, with the figure falling to 11% for those aged between 3 and 6. [193]

Kela, the Finnish Government agency that sets benefits, states in 2017, on its website that

> 'The care allowance is not affected by the family's income. Care allowance is paid separately for every child eligible for the allowance. The care allowance amounts to €338.34 per month for one child under 3 years of age, €101.29 per month for each additional child under 3 years of age, and €65.09 per month for each child over 3 years of age but under school age'.[194]

Care supplement

The Finnish care supplement depends on the size and gross income of the family. The maximum amount of care supplement is €181.07 per month. It is paid for one child only.'[195]

---

[193] Ministry of Social Affairs and Health (2013) *Child and family policy in Finland.* Helsinki. http://www.congreso.es/docu/docum/ddocum/dosieres/sleg/legislatura_10/spl_78/pdfs/41.pdf

[194] http://www.kela.fi/web/en

[195] http://www.kela.fi/web/en/child-benefit

In addition, families in Finland may be eligible for a municipal supplement, and all families receive child benefit, at a comparable rate to the UK for the first child, but then increasing with subsequent children, whereas in the UK, the amount decreases with subsequent children. What is noticeable about this system is that in effect the government is paying a primary carer if they choose to stay at home with a child. Payments continue until the child goes to a municipal nursery or to school. There is no pressure to send children to nurseries; it is a choice.[196]

Compare the situation in Finland with that in the UK, where income support is available if all five of the following conditions are met:

1. Pregnant, or a carer, or a lone parent to a child under five (or in some cases, unable to work due to illness or disability).
2. Aged between 16 and pension qualifying age.
3. On a low income or no income, and less than £16,000 in savings.
4. Work less than 16 hours a week.
5. Live in England, Scotland or Wales.

The amount of income support depends on circumstances, but a parent who is not earning, would be able to claim, in 2017, around £60 per week plus housing benefit and a reduction in council tax; a shockingly low income for someone who cannot work because they have young children. As yet Universal Credit has not been fully rolled out in the UK, but initial assessments show in 2017 that it is unlikely to improve on current provision and may even make matters worse.

Given that Finland, like the UK, also has similar housing allowances, the difference in income levels is stark. It may also partly account for the fact that

[196] http://www.kela.fi/documents/10180/1978560/2015_Home_family2.pdf

Unicef's League Table of Child Well-being in the richest countries of the world, placed Finland 4th overall, and 2nd for material well-being, whilst the UK came 16th, behind countries such as Slovenia, the Czech Republic and Portugal, and 14th for material well-being.[197]

Lone parents in work, as we have seen, are some of the poorest parents in the UK. Even where there are partners in low income families, many of the non-caring parents will be unemployed, on Employment and Support Allowance (ESA) or low wages. It may, then, be appropriate to reconsider an idea that dates back to the 18th century, the social dividend, or citizens wage. A similar concept is 'basic income'. In 2015, the Royal Society for the Encouragement of Arts, Manufactures and Commerce (the RSA) published their report advocating the innovation of a universal basic income.[198] This would be paid to all citizens whether in work or out of work, and which would replace our welfare system. It is argued that a standard flat payment made to every citizen would help reduce poverty traps caused by the benefit system, improve the lot of those in work, and improve fairness.

One scenario at 2013 rates, would see each adult paid £3,692 a year or £71 a week, with children also receiving a payment corresponding roughly to child benefit. Pensioners would be paid a citizen's pension of £7,420 a year. More recently the RSA has looked at comparisons with Universal Credit and the introduction of the National Living Wage. The calculations are complex, but worth the reader's attention, and can be accessed online on the RSA's website.[199] Essentially it is suggested that the increased revenue provided to all citizens up to an income threshold of £75,000, would not only provide

---

[197] https://www.unicef-irc.org/publications/pdf/rc11_eng.pdf

[198] RSA (2015) Creative citizen, creative state - the principled and pragmatic case for a universal basic income.

[199] www.thersa.org

greater income, flexibility and stability to low income families but would also be a net saving to the state through the reduction in personpower and infrastructure required to deliver our current complex benefit system. There have been those who have argued that basic income could act as a disincentive to work, but there is evidence from pilot studies that this is not the case, and Canada is also, in 2016, trialling a basic income model, along with pilots in Italy, the Netherlands, Finland and possibly France.[200]

The greatest aid

Ultimately the biggest driver of need and the consequent gate-keeping requirement for risk-assessed services, is poverty. In the UK, in 2014-2015, 3.9 million children were living in poverty which amounts to more than a quarter of our children.[201] In the Netherlands, which came top in Unicef's League Table of Child Well-being, the figure is around 12%, less than half the UK rate.[202]

In international comparisons with other rich nations, the UK again lags behind and once again it is the Nordic countries which lead the way.[203]

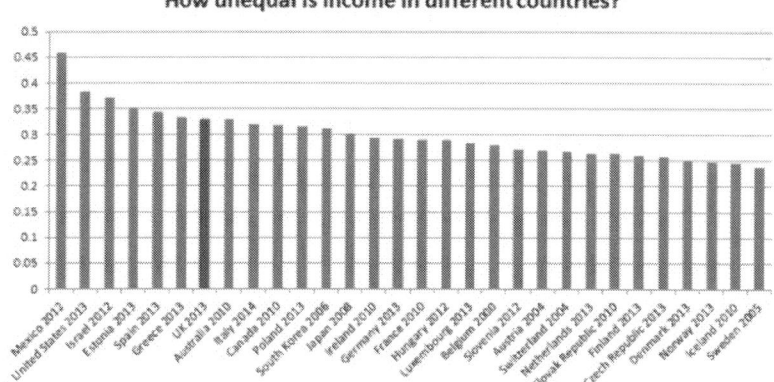

How unequal is income in different countries?

[203] https://www.equalitytrust.org.uk/scale-economic-inequality-uk, accessed 27/1/2017
Luxembourg Income Study http://www.lisdatacenter.org. accessed 27/1/2017

In a nutshell, wealth inequality means being unable to access the services (let alone goods) that the majority in your country can. It means being unable to afford counselling, babysitters, nannies, holidays, dentistry, glasses, safe cars, public transport, sports clubs, private schools, swimming pools, housing in nice areas, good schools and an endless list of things that the other 60% of the nation take for granted. It means having to beg for help to the state, it means allowing the state to set the parameters of what you can and cannot do if you want its help, It means therefore, running the risk that in seeking help from it, it will take the children.

KEY FINDINGS

1) It is predominantly the children of the poor who are in care yet there is no evidence that their parents pose more risk.

2) Income determines agency and options, such as childcare, good schools, aspirations, secure housing, counselling. Those with no or low incomes are assessed by social workers.

3) Domestic violence, substance misuse, poor mental health and psychosis can all be addressed through relatively inexpensive public health approaches.

4) Wherever remotely feasible, women should not be imprisoned but rather serve community sentences, with provision made to ensure that they can continue to parent free from addictions and away from former criminal acquaintances or controllers.

5) Policy change is needed to ensure that a main carer wage is paid, on a sliding scale to account for the number of children aged under 5, disability etc which is forfeited only when the main carer income exceeds a certain threshold; or to ensure a citizens' wage or a Finnish-type model of wage.

QUESTIONS FOR DISCUSSION

(a) What other public health initiatives might meet the needs of parents addicted to drugs or alcohol?
(b) How can public health policy ensure that fathers take financial and emotional responsibility for their children and is it what women want?
(c) What public health initiatives might reduce the prevalence of domestic violence, particularly amongst men?

CHAPTER FIVE

THE CURRENT LEGISLATIVE FRAMEWORK

The Core Features

Under the 1948 Act, a local authority had a duty to receive a child into care if neglect or abuse was evident. In 1952, local authorities gained the power to investigate neglect. Crucially, in 1963, local authorities were given the power to take preventive action. What does this mean?

Legislation in the UK contains both powers and duties. A 'power' is enabling; it means that a local authority can do something. A 'duty', however, is much stronger; the local authority 'must' do certain things where that is stated in the legislation. Thus we can already see that the Children Act 1989 built on what was by then (1989) a century of Victorian thinking about the child. It placed duties on the local authority to place a child into care, but no **duty** on a local authority to take preventive action; only a power. The 1989 Children Act, section 17, continues the power. There is no duty to prevent anything: poverty, poor health, alcoholism, etc. This is consistent with the Poor Laws which have governed our country in various guises for centuries, and which were formally codified by Elizabeth 1 in 1601. In other words, for over 400 years parishes and later local authorities have had the power to support the poor in their areas (but not necessarily those who come from outside their area) but no **duty** to provide for them.

The current legislative framework for working with children and families is set by the Children Act 1989, and whilst later Acts amend or add to it, the 1989 Act's essential tenets still hold.

The core principle of the Act, as set out in Section 1(1) is *the welfare of the child.*

> 's1(1) When a court determines any question with respect to -
> (a) the upbringing of a child; or
> (b) the administration of a child's property or the application of any income arising from it,
> the *child's welfare shall be the court's paramount consideration.'*

The 'welfare principle', as it is known, is further defined in the checklist under s1(3) Children's Act 1989, and must take account of:

1. The wishes and feelings of the child concerned
2. The child's physical, emotional and educational needs
3. The likely effect on the child if circumstances changed as a result of the court's decision
4. The child's age, sex, backgrounds and any other characteristics which will be relevant to the court's decision
5. Any harm the child has suffered or may be at risk of suffering
6. Capability of the child's parents (or any other person the courts find relevant) to meet the child's needs
7. The powers available to the court in the given proceedings

This approach underpins all current legislation in respect of children, with case law further defining what those 'best interests' and welfare of the child might be.[204]

In 1992, the UK ratified the United Nations Convention on the Rights of the Child, and of note here are three Articles:

> Article 3: The best interest of the child should be a primary concern in decisions affecting them.
> Article 6: The right to life and development.
> Article 12: The right for a child's views to be taken into account.

In addition, the Human Rights Act 1998 sets out five rights that underpin our children and family legislation:

> Article 5: The right to liberty and security of person.
> Article 6: The right to a fair trial.
> Article 8: The right to respect for private and family life, home and correspondence.
> Article 10: The right to freedom of expression.
> Article 12: The right to freedom from discrimination in the delivery of these rights.

Before looking more closely at the import of these provisions, which at first glance seem so right and necessary, it is worth remembering that once dreamed up and ratified, countries and individuals tend not to think outside the box. As a result, it is hard to draw international comparisons with wealthy countries that have different legislative frameworks for child and family law, as they have all, for the most part, gone down the same narrow alleyway.

---

[204] See, for example, Lord Justice Munby's ruling: https://www.law.ox.ac.uk/sites/files/oxlaw/a5-herring-redefining-childrens-welfare.pdf. https://www.solicitorsjournal.com/news/family/children/judge-children's-welfare-'-standards-2012'-munby-lj-says-ultra-orthodox-ruling

As we shall see with the various Human Rights Act articles, rights are always qualified and to those on the receiving end, sometimes seemingly vacuous. Liberty, the UK charity concerned with human rights, gives a good example of this -

> 'Article 8 is a qualified right and as such the right to a private and family life and respect for the home and correspondence may be limited. So while the right to privacy is engaged in a wide number of situations, the right may be lawfully limited. Any limitation must have regard to the fair balance that has to be struck between the competing interests of the individual and of the community as a whole.

In particular any limitation must be:

> in accordance with law; necessary and proportionate; and for one or more of the following legitimate aims:
> - the interests of national security;
> - the interests of public safety or the economic well-being of the country;
> - the prevention of disorder or crime;
> - the protection of health or morals; or
> - the protection of the rights and freedoms of others.'[205]

Human Rights and Compliance?

The exact wording of Article 3 of the United Nations Convention on the Rights of the Child is –

---

[205] https://www.liberty-human-rights.org.uk/human-rights/what-are-human-rights/human-rights-act/article-8-right-private-and-family-life, accessed 28/1/2017

'1. In all actions concerning children, whether undertaken by public or private social welfare institutions, courts of law, administrative authorities or legislative bodies, the best interests of the child shall be **a** primary consideration'.

In the Children Act 1989, the child's best interests were changed from the Convention's '**a** primary consideration' to '**the** paramount consideration'. This chapter will argue that this change of emphasis, the use of the definite and singular consideration, as opposed to the Convention's more general use of the indefinite article 'a', has led to seeking only the child's best interests, and in turn, in part, to the calamitously high number of children in care and a total disregard for the wider family.

Many children are taken away from their parents at birth, when a mother literally cannot physically let alone mentally defend herself. A 2015 study found that at least 24 per cent of women whose children, many of them babies, were taken into care, were likely to return to court, having previously appeared as a respondent in section 31 (Care) proceedings, and that the proportion increases to almost one in every three for women aged between sixteen and nineteen.[206] The same research also notes that although there is provision for post adoption support for these parents, it is rarely provided in a meaningful way. Like other UNCRC signatories, such as Australia, Canada or the USA, there is no statutory mandate for the provision of tailored services to parents to enable them not only

---

[206] Broadhurst K, Alrouh B, Yeend E, Harwin J, Shaw M, Pilling M, Mason C & Kershaw S (2015) Connecting Events in Time to Identify a Hidden Population: Birth Mothers and Their Children in Recurrent Care Proceedings in England. *British Journal of Social Work.* 45(8): 2241-2260

to survive the trauma of having children taken away, but to 'rehabilitate' them so that the need does not arise again.

Broadhurst et al (2015) note that

> 'Although birth parents are entitled to post-adoption support under the 2002 Adoption and Children Act, services are highly variable, take-up is inconsistent (Neil et al., 2010) and 'there is no evidence that support in its current form meets the complex needs of this higher-risk population....evidence from this study indicates that a sizeable percentage of women reappear because their problems are repeated rather than resolved. Here, an expectation of natural recovery fails this group—evidence is that women do return to court, sometimes multiple times, losing successive infants to public care and adoption.'[207]

This is just one facet of how an over zealous and single-minded approach to the child, rather than to the child and its wider family, can serve only to increase the numbers in care.

Following publication of the Broadhurst study (2015), *Community Care,* the online journal for social workers, reported its findings. One commentator posted the following -

> 'I've read the article, and the responses. I've also lived it first hand. In 1998, I was 22, I had just split with my

---

[207] Broadhurst K et al (2015) *op cit.* p.

husband, the father of all 3 of my children, ages 1,2 & 3 years old. It was a very difficult time for me. Yet I struggled through, with little family support, and little money, I was the best parent I could be. But I suffered from post natal depression that had not been diagnosed. The "baby blues" I had with my 3rd child, just never went away, like it did with my first 2 children. I think the breakdown of my marriage contributed to that too. I asked social services for help. Temporary respite care 1 weekend out of every 6, would have helped me get back on track. Instead, my social worker provoked me after I asked for help, and they had my children in their care. So I snapped and slapped her. I know violence is wrong, I'm not a violent person, but the social worker really brought out the worst in me. She would criticise me as a mother, make demands of me that were just too unreasonable, and pick holes in me . . . she lied about how I treated my children, etc etc, and her position of power and authority, I couldn't defend myself. I lost all 3 children. I haven't seen them from that day to this. 4 years later, I had another baby. I was ready, and happy to be a mum again. Social services spent my entire pregnancy plotting and planning behind my back. They didn't assess me, write to me, visit me or telephone me. They showed up in the room I gave birth in, 2 hours after she was born, and took her from the hospital, in the middle of the night, and didn't tell me until after she was already gone, with an invalid court order. That was in Nov 2001. I haven't seen her since. In 2005, I gave birth to a healthy boy. He's still with me. We were placed in an assessment centre for 12 weeks, 40 miles away from my home, family and friends. I passed my assessment. My son is nearly 11, he's healthy and happy, he wishes for nothing, he has everything. Including a mama who adores him. He's never been allowed to meet his older siblings. In court, all 4 of my first children were force adopted, my consent to adoption was dispensed with. I was nothing but an invisible baby making machine. An unpaid surrogate mother for some couple who God didn't see fit to bless with children. And after? I was left to get on with it. Pick up the pieces of my life and put them back together alone. With no help. No support. No counselling. . .The police arrested me for the original social workers allegations, but surprise surprise, all charges against me were dropped. Lack of evidence proves evidence of absence. Yet I never got even one of my children back. Tell me, how is any of it right?'[208]

There are innovative organisations that are attempting to step into this lacuna in preventative and support services. The Family Drug and Alcohol Court National Unit (www.fdac.org.uk) tries to adopt a problem solving, non-adversarial approach to family justice and to help parents to acquire the skills they need to avoid repeats of children being taken into care. Similarly, Pause (www.pause.org.uk) tries to enable women to recover after child removal, and to do the job that arguably should have been done by social workers long before the child was born/removed, and in any case, most certainly afterwards to avoid repetition. These are organisations that are dealing in one way or another with the aftermath. What is needed is a much more holistic approach which would take as its starting

[208]http://www.communitycare.co.uk/2015/12/14/mothers-lose-children-care-proceedings-offered-little-support-report-says/ accessed 29/1/2017

point, an alteration to s1(1) of the Children Act 1989, so that the 'welfare of the child ***and family***' is '***a*** paramount consideration'.

The best interests of the child and its family

By widening the definition of the welfare principle, to include the family and child, the court would have to pay due consideration to the needs of the family both in terms of preventing 'significant harm' (the threshold that justifies intervention in family life in the 'best interests' of children, as per Section 31(2) of the Children Act 1989 -

> (2) A court may only make a care order or supervision order if it is satisfied—
>
> (a) that the child concerned is suffering, or is likely to suffer, significant harm; and
>
> (b) that the harm, or likelihood of harm, is attributable to —
>
> (i) the care given to the child, or likely to be given to him if the order were not made, not being what it would be reasonable to expect a parent to give to him; or
>
> (ii) the child's being beyond parental control.

An example of how the law could be reformulated might be -

(2) A court may only make a care order or supervision order if it is satisfied -

(a) that the child concerned is suffering, or is likely to suffer, significant harm; and

(b) That the harm, or likelihood of harm cannot be diminished by -

(i) The exclusion of any secondary carer from the home where domestic violence, symbiotic drug/alcohol use or other co-dependence exists; and

146

(ii) The provision, by Order, of services to the child and/or his family; and

(iii) Such services to include the provision of drug or alcohol rehabilitation, counselling, financing of au pair, psychiatric care, housing and financial support in kind.

As we have seen, S.17 of the Children Act 1989 merely enables local authorities to support children in need in a non-specific way. Reformulating S.31 (and other linked Sections) to force the Court to consider the wider family and social context would not only provide the support needed in the home, but also obviate the need for such large numbers in care at a huge cost to the public purse but more importantly, to future lives and generations. It would break the cycle.

One other lacuna might also be filled. When a case comes to the Family Court (a subject dealt with in more detail later) the Judge is ruling on the basis of the facts outlined to him by the plaintiff (usually the local authority) and the defendant (usually the parent/s). In addition, social workers would need not only to be more specifically trained to a higher and more professional standard, but also to submit reports to the Court upon which safe judgments could be made.

For example, in the case of Z-O'C (Children) [2014] EWCA Civ 1808, which concerned an appeal against Supervision Orders, it was noted that:

> 'The underlying concern had been one of long-term neglect which was said to be the result of a lack of

parenting capacity and low motivation. At trial the
local authority sought care orders for both children,
planning for the elder child to remain living with
grandparents and for the younger to be adopted. The
trial judge had had three pieces of written evidence
before him: (i) a psychological assessment which
concluded that motivation could not be measured,
but that the father had a capacity to compensate for
the mother's need for support, and that there was a
possibility that the parents could "enhance their
parental skills to a level that would allow good
enough parenting"; (ii) a negative parenting
assessment which appeared to have been compiled
without the authors having had sight of much
relevant material; and (iii) the report by the
children's guardian who had been appointed late
and had only met with the parents once and
observed contact once.'[209]

Learning from other countries

In 2002, as part of the Scottish Executive's review of child
protection, an international seminar was held which highlighted the
differences between us, other English speaking nations such as
Australia and Canada, and countries such as Belgium, Sweden and
France. Key amongst the differences is the way in which the legal
framework and social service provision focuses not just on the child

---

[209] http://www.familylawweek.co.uk/site.aspx?i=ed143389, accessed 31/1/2017

but on the family and social context. The seminar elicited the following differences:[210]

Countries covered at Seminar	England, Scotland, Australia, Canada	Belgium, Sweden, France, Germany
Type of welfare state	Tendency to residual and selective provision	Tendency to comprehensive and universal provision
Place of child protection services	Separated from family support services	Embedded within and normalised by broad child welfare or public health services
Type of child protection system	Legal, bureaucratic, investigative, adversarial	Voluntary, flexible, solution focussed, collaborative
Orientation to children and families	Emphasis on individual children's rights. Professionals primary responsibility is for the child's welfare.	Emphasis on family unity. Professionals usually work with the family as a whole.
Basis of the service	Investigating risk in order to formulate child safety plans.	Supportive or therapeutic responses to meeting needs or resolving problems.

[210]International perspectives on child protection: Report of a semindar held on 20 March 2002. Part of the Scottish Excecutive's Child Protection Review. Page 5. http://www.gov.scot/resource/doc/1181/0009926.pdf, accessed 2/2/2017

Countries covered at Seminar	England, Scotland, Australia, Canada	Belgium, Sweden, France, Germany
Coverage	Resources are concentrated on familied where risks of (re)abuse are immediate and high.	Resources are available to more families at an earlier stage.

This difference in approach is embedded in a wider policy context. For example, Sweden and Belgium have child protection 'systems' that are rooted in a policy context of providing social assistance and public services on a comprehensive basis. As a result, specialist services build on the foundations of universal general provision, and draw on greater good will towards social workers and their equivalents than tends to be the case in the UK, Canada or Australia.[211]

This difference in approach is further demonstrated in the 2002 report to the Scottish Executive.[212]

---

[211] International perspectives on child protection: Report of a semindar held on 20 March 2002. Part of the Scottish Excecutive's Child Protection Review. Page 5. http://www.gov.scot/resource/doc/1181/0009926.pdf, accessed 2/2/2017

[212] op cit. p.7

Differences between British/American & Belgian Systems

	UK/American Systems	Belgian System
General welfare state approach	Residual	Universal
State-citizen basis	Individualism	Solidarity
View of child abuse	Resulting from pathology	Linked to common social and parenting problems
Approach to child abuse	Authoritarian and punishment orientated	Helping families
Context for dealing with concerns	Expectation to report cases and deal with families in segregated ways.	Confidentiality and health promotion
Response to referrals	Investigation and collation of information	Immediate help

Ontario and Sweden Compared[213]

Ontario	Sweden
Standardised assessments and actions	Flexible assessments and actions
Assessment is flexible	Assessment is psycho-social

---

[213] *op cit.* p.11

Ontario	Sweden
Prime focus is to investigate risk and safety	Prime focus is to understand problems and needs
Emphasis on legal authority and regular use of court orders to secure parental co-operation or alternative care	Emphasis on professional authority and voluntary co-operation with parents
The overriding concern is to achieve change so that child is safer	Building relationships with all family members is crucial

Whilst we may want to argue over the distinctions made in the above tables, it is nonetheless clear that other countries have a more preventative, public health
approach, which has largely been ignored in the UK; responses to various sensational cases leading inexorably to a further tightening of the belt and a stronger forensic, risk assessed and investigative approach.

That is not to say that any one other country has the answer. Any search of the internet will provide numerous examples of anomalies and legal cases in the European Court of Human Rights. But it does hint at how we might better frame our legislation. A change in the Children Act 1989 and in particular, replacing s1(1) of the Children Act 1989, so that the welfare of the child is not the paramount consideration but so that, rather, the 'welfare of the child _and family_' is '_a_ paramount consideration' would not only provide child protection and family courts with a better and wider consideration of the contexts involved, but would also act to encourage a policy shift towards more holistic working; something which has been at the core of much policy and academic thinking over the decades but which has been largely ignored by successive governments.[214]

What do we mean by harm?

Under Section 31 of the Children Act 1989, a care order can be made if the Court is satisfied that a child 'is suffering or is likely to suffer' significant harm, and it is attributable to the care given to the child not being what it would be reasonable to expect a parent to give, or the child is beyond parental control.

The statutory definition in the Children Act 1989 states that 'harm' means ill-treatment or impairment of health and development. In turn, ill-treatment includes sexual abuse and non physical abuse such as emotional abuse or neglect. Health' includes both physical and mental health, and 'development' includes physical, intellectual, emotional, social and behavioural development. In determining whether health or development have been impaired the Act suggests a comparison between the health or development of the child in question 'with that which could reasonably be expected of a similar child'.

Under the Adoption and Children Act 2002, the definition of 'significant harm' was widened to include 'impairment suffered from seeing or hearing the ill-treatment of another' in order to include witnessing domestic and other violence. If, after a child protection investigation under section 47 of the Children Act 1989, it is decided that the threshold of significant harm has been reached, a Care Order

---

[214] BULLOCK Roger, et al.(1995) Child protection: messages from research. Department of Health, London: HMSO

may be sought under section 31. In considering the options available to the Court, the Court will then consider the welfare of the child as its paramount consideration. It will not and does not consider the welfare of the child in care, because the Court deals only with the case before it. Thus the option to consider whether care is likely to cause 'significant harm' is not of interest.

This is an important point, because we have seen that children in care are at risk of significant harm through constant moves in care, the breaking of bonds of attachment with their primary and other family carers, abuse within care, and the lack of locus when they enter the adult world with no family back up, context or familial preparation for it.

There is another danger, namely, that the impact of certain types of parenting on a child will differ from child to child, and the Court is making judgments based not on any evidence but on what it believes is likely to be the case. Many wealthier parents, unaffected by social work interference, will have had a negative impact on aspects of their children's welfare. This is because some parents are insensitive to their children's needs, or are perceived to be: the father who shouts at his children, which doesn't affect the eldest two, but which damages the third child who cannot cope with aggression. The ambitious parents, whose subtle academic pressure can be linked to the onset of anxiety, depression or eating disorders. The busy career parents, who have no time in the week for warm proactive parenting. The divorcing parents - where Dad's leaving for another woman leaves the children feeling second best, and where the mother is destroyed. There are thousands of ways in which we can cause our children 'significant harm' but most of us do not fall under the lens of social services, and most of us survive our parents' errors and failings because the context of our wider lives, within the family, community and school gives us a certain safety net and grounding. The child in care lacks all of these.

The fact that 'is suffering, or is likely to suffer, significant harm' is the threshold for a Care Order is a cause for concern not only because we do not, in all honesty, know - even in some of the worst cases - whether the child will suffer, or whether it will be worse off in care, but also because what we perceive as harmful is relative. For example, in the UK, France, Belgium, Canada. Finland and many other countries, homeschooling is legal. However, in Sweden, homeschooling has only been allowed in very restricted circumstances and is not approved where the grounds are religious or philosophical. In 2009 a child, Domenic Johansson, was taken from his parents, Christopher Johansson, a Swedish citizen, and Annie Johansson, from India) when they were on board a Turkish Air Flight 990. Domenic was taken into police custody on the basis that he had been homeschooled. He was just 7 years old. His parents said that he had been homeschooled because they had planned to leave Sweden shortly and he was only just of school age. Despite legal appeals, Domenic is still in care. He has reportedly not been allowed to see his parents for five and a half years despite the fact that the Swedish District Court agreed in 2012, that his parents took good care of him.[215][216]

This is not to comment on the rights or wrongs of that particular case, but merely to point out that the 'significant harm' in this case, was the parents' decision to homeschool, which Sweden opposes and

[215] https://en.m.wikipedia.org/wiki/Homeschooling_international_status_and_statistics

[216] https://adfinternational.org/detailspages/case-details/johannson-v.-sweden

sees as dangerous to any child. In the UK it is legal and not considered damaging to children.

There are many facets to parenting, and not all fit neatly with textbook ideas about what constitutes good parenting. I was brought up in the 1950s, when it was common for parents to hit or slap a child, and when teachers frequently walloped children in the classroom, in front of other children. Now we - generally the liberal middle class - think differently. We think that the sort of behaviour that we all witnessed in the Fifties is tantamount to 'significant harm'. We advocate authoritative parenting, parenting which explains to a child why something is wrong, which is warm and affectionate and which praises good behaviour and ignores, or finds subtle ways of dealing with poor behaviour. Following the Children Act 2004, it is now illegal to smack a child hard enough to leave a mark. Most of us think this right, but there are many parents in the UK who have been brought up differently, and in different cultures, and who believe that it did them no harm. They, like us, will generally parent as they themselves were parented unless something happens to make them think differently. It is one of the reasons why children from poorer homes tend to have more behavioural problems in school; they simply cannot understand the teacher's more educated, liberal, authoritative approach. They are used to being told sharply to stop doing something, and struggle from a young age to even comprehend the middle class approach to discipline.[217]

---

[217] See, for example, Department for Education (2012) *Pupil behaviour in schools in England*. RR218

The fact that we cannot universally agree upon what actions definitively lead to a child 'suffering, or . . . likely to suffer, significant harm',[218] is surely a matter of concern. The Children Act 2004 is at least clear about one stated action, smacking that leaves a mark. The same might be said about the Adoption and Children Act 2002, which amended s.31 of the Children Act 1989, to include the witnessing of domestic violence –

> In section 31 of the 1989 Act (care and supervision orders), at the end of the definition of "harm" in subsection (9) there is inserted 'including, for example, impairment suffered from seeing or hearing the ill-treatment of another'.

This Act, together with the Domestic Violence, Crime and Victims Act 2004, as amended by the Domestic Violence, Crime and Victims (Amendment) Act 2012 which includes 'causing or allowing serious physical harm (equivalent to grievous bodily harm) to a child or vulnerable adult', and s.76 of the Serious Crime Act 2015 come together to provide a new offence of "controlling or coercive behaviour in an intimate or family relationship". The new offence thus closes a gap in the law around psychological and emotional abuse that stops short of physical abuse and can carry a prison sentence or fine.

It remains questionable whether even these seemingly obviously harmful types of parenting actually lead to harm that is greater than the harm done by placing a child in care. The answer surely lies in public health strategies that punish or rehabilitate the perpetrator rather than punishing the victim, the child and - more often than not - the mother.

---

[218] Children Act 1989, s.47(1)(b)

We have not yet touched on the vagaries of 'emotional abuse', or 'neglect', but what we can say is that however heinous such parenting is, can we be sure that in placing a child into care, we are not making matters worse? Given what we know about care (see Chapter 3), how can we be sure that however bad such parenting is, care is not worse? All the evidence points the other way. Is it not better and safer to work with the parent/s in ensuring change and to spend resources on that, rather than on care?

Avoiding Care Proceedings

When a referral is made or abuse suggested, an initial assessment will be made and the matter may be dropped, or may trigger support and assessment as a 'child in need' under s.17 of the Children Act. In these circumstances, assessment using the Common Assessment Framework, which adopts an ecological - wider than nuclear family - approach will be needed to identify needs and provision. Again, according to Government guidance (2015) the child's wishes and feelings should be sought and the child interviewed away from its parents. Whilst on paper this seems sensible, in reality many parents would baulk at their child being asked questions in their absence. Neither they nor the child have committed a criminal offence, yet in criminal law usual practice if a child has committed an offence, would be for the police to request a parent to attend the interview. Further, whilst a child considered capable may be interviewed during care or child protection proceedings, there is no requirement to explain to that child their human rights, nor is it clear what they are.

If there is concern that the threshold of 'is suffering or is likely to suffer significant harm'(s.47 of Children Act 1989) is being crossed, the local authority may hold a strategy discussion to share information and decide how best to deal with any child protection concerns. At this point child protection concerns may still be dropped (as indeed they may following a child protection conference) and the child may revert to being 'a child in need' of support. As a minimum, the strategy discussion should involve the child's social worker and manager, a police representative, and a health professional. Ideally others including early years or teaching staff should also be involved. The strategy discussion may take the form of a multi-agency meeting or be done over the phone.

Government guidance[219] again deliberately places the interests of the state over those of the family –

'(The strategy discussion) decides what information should be shared with   the child and family (on the basis that information is not shared if this may jeopardise a police investigation or place the child at risk of significant harm'.[220]

A statement of the seemingly obvious, but one which, because as we have seen 'significant harm' is in the eye of the beholder, means that essentially information will not be shared if the authorities would prefer not to.

At this crucial information-gathering stage, where a decision is about to be made as to the next course of action, parents are not invited to the discussion. This is critical because the professionals will have

---

[219] HM Government (2015) *Working together to safeguard children: A guide to inter-agency working to safeguard and promote the welfare of children.*

[220] *Op.cit* p. 37

together formed a view. Neither parent, advocate nor wider family are invited to put their views. It is akin to school playground bullying, where a group of people, some of whom you thought were friendly towards you, get in a corner of the playground and clearly talk about you, refuse to let you join in, and then tell you that you can come to their next meeting.

Improving the approach

A more positive and collaborative approach might involve some initial preparation before the strategy discussion. For example, two weeks before the strategy discussion, the local authority might send a proforma letter to the parents, which clearly and unambiguously sets out the concerns and invites the parent/s to respond to each point at the strategy discussion, with the support of an advocate. Such advocates should be independent, trained and readily available to any parent. Government guidance should make it clear that parents must bring a trained children and families independent advocate with them to all meetings. It is essential because questioning parents about their capacity to parent, will inflame emotions. Solution focused work - the essence of work with children and families - means that all parties should be enabled to visualise a way forward. Because it is a strategy discussion (and not a child protection case conference) it might also help to have an independent facilitator or chair. If parents are to be kept on board, and if partnership and working together is to have any meaning, parents must not feel threatened; but must be equal partners.

Strategy discussions that involve all key players in this way, and which also adopt a public health perspective - by which I mean proper and timely support for parents' own addictions/mental health/housing/ vulnerability - may then be able to deflect any need for child protection measures. There is no point in paying lip service to the inclusion of other professionals and agencies, such as the police or housing, if they have only come to the meeting to express an opinion. The lead professional must not only tell the parents what their main concerns are, including concerns about the parents themselves, but also the other agencies/professionals. Professionals are being invited to engage in the strategy in order to find a solution not just to the child's problems, but to the wider ecosystem in which that child lives. Thus the lead needs to be aware of what could be done, for example, to improve benefits take up, housing, schooling, risk of domestic violence, parental mental and physical health, and so on and must ensure that all professionals involved in the strategy discussion are clear about the problems and how they could address them. All too often, at present, a teacher in a strategy discussion may comment on a child's disruptive behaviour with no onus on the teacher to have referred that child to an educational psychologist. A housing officer may report that the parents are about to be evicted for non-payment of rent with no onus on that housing officer to have looked at whether the parents have debt/ benefit problems that could be resolved with the right support. There is simply no point in backing vulnerable parents into a corner and turning on the headlights.

Ultimately, however, if it is thought that there are child protection concerns that next meeting is likely to be a case conference. In the meantime, s.47 inquiries will begin, with the social worker taking the lead on a full assessment. Government guidance (2015) mentions involving the family, but it makes it clear that assessments of the situation should actually be assessments of the child. Paragraph 35 states that –

> 'High quality assessments: are child-centred. Where there is a conflict of interest, decisions should be made in the child's best interests;'[221]

The Case Conference

Although even at the earlier stages of case conferences and strategy meetings, parents should receive information about advocacy support and their case, they are often, by this point, confused, angry and isolated. Organisations such as Family Rights Group can be a great help, but many parents do not know of them, and outside London, physical support in terms of advocacy is limited in its availability. Moreover although parent/s are normally invited to case conferences (which occur prior to any care proceedings) local authorities can exclude a parent where they believe that there is good reason (such as domestic violence) to do so.

Children who are considered mature enough to voice an opinion, can be invited to case conferences and give their views to the Court (supported by a Cafcass appointed Guardian) and will be prepared for this by the social worker or Guardian. Under the Children Act 1989, because the welfare of the child is paramount, the child's interests become separated from those of the family or parent/s. A child considered mature enough, therefore, will be asked to assume

---

[221] HM Government (2015) *Working together to safeguard children: A guide to inter-agency working to safeguard and promote the welfare of children.* https://www.gov.uk/government/uploads/system/uploads/attachment_data/file/419595/Working_Together_to_Safeguard_Children.pdf accessed 15/2/2017

responsibility for indicating what the problems are, or where he/she wishes to live. No child, other than those going to kinship carers, however, knows what the future will hold for him/her in the care system. Most have simply no idea of the potential implications of what they say.

Case conferences are usually called by social services, or occasionally by the NSPCC, where abuse is suspected or 'confirmed'. They usually take place before care proceedings are commenced, and may obviate the need for them if a satisfactory outcome can be arranged. The essence of case conferences is that they should involve all interested parties and agencies involved with the child (although not necessarily with the parent) so that information is shared and an accurate picture formed

It sounds sensible, but in reality case conferences are inevitably hostile experiences for parents, as they tend to concentrate on the welfare of the child and therefore on the perceived failings of the parent/s. Birmingham City Council carried out research into how child protection services were perceived by parents and staff. Their report comments -

'To parents, conferences are a daunting prospect and are ultimately a hostile, intimidating environment where potentially life shattering decisions are taken by officials they don't know. . . Too often parents were ill prepared because they did not receive a report in time or at all, minutes were not translated into actions quick enough, language was inaccessible, there was no pre-meeting with the social[222] worker or the conference chair' (Birmingham City Council 2014).

Quintessentially, the English and Welsh child protection scheme is adversarial and inquisitorial. Despite the best efforts in government guidance to embrace ideas such as working in partnership, or 'empowerment', because there is no holistic family/public health approach in the first instance, proceedings are liable to hostility/ defensiveness and resentment.

Worse, in my own experience, assessments may be done by trainee social work students or poorly trained social workers, yet still these will be defended because professionals often see it as their duty to uphold the decision of a fellow professional. Many of them - teachers, health visitors, GPs, police officers - have other busy lives. They are not going to spend much time dissecting just how good any one assessment is. The parent knows, and may sit fuming, but can say little for fear of making things worse. They are disempowered precisely because the narrow focus on the welfare of the child means that the child's interests are represented by the state (in the form of social workers, guardians and other professionals), and all key players are on the same team; there can be no meaningful place for parents, siblings or the wider family. Ultimately, the system is wrongly geared, and if we really want to improve outcomes for children and families in the immediate and long term, we must totally rethink how we approach child protection.

---

[222] Birmingham City Council Strategic Research Team (2014) *Child protection research: Parents' experiences of the child protection process and and staff experience of working with parents: A qualitative study.* https://www.rip.org.uk/assets/_userfiles/files/Publications_resources/Parents'%20experiences%20of%20the%20child%20protection%20process.pdf , *accessed 24/2/2017*

The disabling effect of poverty

As we have seen, it is often not risk of 'significant harm' but rather poverty that brings parents under the spotlight of social services, sadly often because the parent/s have gone to them for help. Those better off, know better. But it is salutary here to remember how the impact of poverty is ongoing and can seriously undermine a parent's capacity to attend, defend or collaborate with proceedings. In 2016, Community Care published this survivor's story:

'Imagine then, if you're a parent with children in the care system at Christmas. To my knowledge, all local authorities provide their foster carers with a specific amount to be put aside for Christmas gifts. In my local authority, North Tyneside, this is £150. I know this because my children, still in the system, tell me. My research however indicates this amount can be as high as £247.67 (Somerset). Residential homes are afforded around the same amount, and presents for children in the care system are also donated from members of the public and businesses through initiatives such as my local Metro Radio's "Cash for Kids". . .All of this is wonderful and richly deserved. No child should go without, particularly not the most vulnerable in our society and I am glad systems are in place. However, for the vast majority of parents who have children in the system, for whatever reason, this can add another layer of stress and anxiety.

When your child is removed from your care, or when your child is voluntarily accommodated by the local authority, you lose all entitlements to benefits for that child. Child benefit is retained for eight weeks; however, child tax credit is removed the day your child leaves your home. If you are in receipt of housing benefit or council

165

tax support, the amount you receive will decrease. If you live in a local authority property, you may now be considered under occupied and your eligible rent covered by housing benefit will again decrease by up to 25% thanks to the controversial "bedroom tax". You can ask children's services to make a payment under s17 CA89 to help you pay your rent during proceedings, but this is not widely known, nor advertised.

If you claim Income Support as a lone parent, when your children are no longer in your care, temporarily or permanently, you lose your entitlement to claim as a parent and must claim Job Seekers Allowance instead. This means you must be "available for work". If you are going through care proceedings and have meetings, conferences, assessment appointments, court hearings and supervised contacts to attend, this makes being "available for work" very difficult indeed. Add the expectation of Christmas gifts into the mix and it makes for an extremely stressful situation during what is unquestionably the worst period of your life.'

The article continues:

'Professor Brid Featherstone, a social work lecturer at the University of Huddersfield, sees poverty as being inextricably linked to rising care applications.
"Unfortunately, since 2010 poverty has been increasing and we are now in the middle of a perfect storm. Years of cuts to family income and council services have devastated family capacities and support services such as children's services."

She says this means cash-strapped councils are increasingly spending their resources on expensive care proceedings, while their support and preventive services become increasingly "hollowed out".'

The article goes on to highlight the reality of how poverty and disempowerment jeopardise a family's right's under article 8 of the Human Rights Act, to a private and family life. The mother explained how -

'I was single, living in a local authority property after spending four months in a women's refuge. I had fled domestic violence, and was in receipt of benefits because my mental health had been in crisis and I was unable to work. The instability of my mental health was also the trigger for the local authority issuing proceedings. I was pregnant with my youngest child and had three children in the care system and one with their father. My eldest son came back to live with me on his 16th birthday after five months in foster care. This meant I could apply for Child Tax Credit as he was in full time education undertaking GCSE's and then A Levels. . . Upon a work capability assessment, it was deemed my mental health was stable enough for me to work and I was no longer eligible for ESA. There was simply no other benefit to claim, I was pregnant and in the middle of care proceedings. From November 2012 until May 2013, when I reached 29 weeks pregnant and could access Income Support for the reminder of my pregnancy, me and my teenage son lived on his child tax credit alone; a total of £51 per week.

Breakfast became a luxury. Lunch and tea became 15p noodles, sometimes with a bit of "Savers" sauce, from the local supermarket. We couldn't afford fruit or vegetables. Through a chilly winter, we went without gas and, consequently, heating. We got used to freezing showers and sat with blankets and hot water bottles. If we ran out of electricity on the meter before we had money to top it up, we did without. It was like both our birthdays had come at once when the food bank delivered us packages. I remember crying when the gentleman delivering it offered me a kind word.

But my son still went to school. He still studied for, sat and passed his GCSEs. My unborn son was still provided for. I sold my underwear online to afford his crib and second-hand blankets. I felt overwhelming shame. Christmas 2012 still had to be paid for, and I was now "competing" with the local authority, who could provide my children's foster carers with enough money to cover the items on "Santa's List". I remember one of my children wanting an expensive Lego set. I begged and borrowed to afford it.

When you're eight, these things matter, and I was desperately trying to overcompensate for the mistakes I had made which had led to him being placed in care. Our family "Christmas" took place in a cold, clinical, contact centre. I had done my best to provide what I could for everyone. The first proceedings concluded, the second were issued upon my new-born son's removal at 6 days old. I was informed by the DWP I was no longer entitled to Income Support because my child was not with me and again could live only on my eldest son's child tax credit.

I could not pay rent, nor council tax and ended up owing thousands of pounds of debt to the same local authority who had taken my baby and was fighting to have him adopted. Some days I could not afford the train fare to get to court. None of this was taken into account by *the local authority when assessing me and, in fact, my need to use a food bank was then presented as evidence of a "chaotic lifestyle".*[223]

The article, published online, elicited many comments - some critical of the mother's lack of good parenting - but perhaps most interesting was this, from a child protection social worker:

As part of the assessments we need to consider the financial implications for return, we spend hundreds of thousands on residential placements, thousands on taxi's, but frown when a parent asks for a bed so that they can have overnight contact with their child.'

This is not the chapter in which to explore further the binds with which poverty ties; it merely points again to the context in which a parent will often face care proceedings.

The lack of statutory duty to involve the wider family or to use Family Group Conferencing

Best Practice Guidance on the Public Law Outline stresses the importance of planning in partnership with the whole family and significant alternative carers at the pre-proceedings stage.[224] Family Group Conferences give families the opportunity to meet together to work out the best possible plan for the child. They can and should be empowering, because the decision makers are the family members,

---

[223] Community Care (2016) http://www.communitycare.co.uk/2016/12/19/services-need-understand-financial-impact-care-proceedings-parents/

[224] Ministry of Justice (2009) *Preparation for care and supervision proceedings: A best practice guide for use buy all professionals involved with children and families pre-proceedings and in preparation for applications made under section 31 of the Children Act 1989.*

including aunts, uncles, parents, grandparents and significant others (to the family), and not the professionals. An independent co-ordinator facilitates the conference, and the decisions that the family and wider family reach, will then need to be agreed with the professionals. It is not a cure-all; but it is an important pre-proceedings tool and one that is sadly not universal or statutory.[225] Moreover, it is frequently used only after care proceedings have begun. In 2016, Alan Johnson MP, former Secretary of State for Education, called on the government both to make FGCs mandatory and to ensure that they are used before care proceedings are started.[226] So far, in a time of public expenditure cuts, their use far from being mandatory, has declined.

The Family Court

Care proceedings are heard in the Family Court, and are based on civil rather than criminal law. There is no jury. In civil law the judge decides from the evidence before him/her, on 'the balance of probabilities' or put simply that the case made 'is more likely than not' to result in harm. Thus parents usually lose the care of their children without any criminal case being brought to court. They are not judged by a jury. By comparison, a man who has stolen money at gun point from a bank and been caught red-handed, is entitled to plead 'not guilty'. He will be tried using our criminal law, which demands that before a defendant can be found guilty, a jury made up from the general public, must be sure 'beyond reasonable doubt', or as judges often say, 'they must be persuaded so that they are sure', that he is guilty. By contrast, the decision made by the Family Court is based on the evidence given by social workers, doctors, 'expert witnesses' (professionals such as

---

[225] For more information on family group conferencing, see www.frg.org.uk

[226] See, for example, http://www.communitycare.co.uk/2016/01/08/family-group-conferences-made-statutory-says-former-education-secretary/

doctors who often make a living from giving evidence based on their expertise) and the parent/s. There is no jury, no need to be sure 'beyond reasonable doubt', but merely the need for one judge to 'believe', on 'the balance of probability - that the case has been made. To find the opposite is to find against fellow 'professionals'.

The local authority, of course, has all the money it needs to take proceedings. In the Army, for example, a soldier facing a court martial is entitled to legal representation from the Army's resources. A criminal, whether rich or poor, is entitled to free legal representation and a trial with a jury for any crime likely to incur a sentence of more than six months. But parent/s have no such right to be heard by a jury and the 'sentence' can be life. There is also no appeal system, no right to take a case to a higher court of appeal, and no right to have the case reviewed or compensation awarded. In the criminal courts, by comparison, a 'defendant' who has lost his appeal against conviction, can try once more via the Criminal Cases Review Commission if he wishes to show that a miscarriage of justice has occurred.[227] Nothing, however, for people who lose their families.

Unless there is an Emergency Protection Order or an immediate need to 'rescue' a child, care proceedings usually start after the local authority has decided that despite their efforts, the child remains at risk. The first step may be a pre-proceedings meeting with the parents and their solicitor to discuss how the care option could be avoided. It's possible even at that point, that a formal agreement may be reached with the parent/s, although breaking of the agreement is likely to result in care proceedings.

---

[227] http://www.ccrc.gov.uk/wp-content/uploads/2015/01/CCRC-Useful-information-for-potential-applicants.pdf , accessed 25/2/2017

Initially often the local authority will apply for an interim care order, which is awarded for eight weeks, but which can be renewed every four weeks. Whilst it is in force, the local authority will be producing a care plan. The care plan can include sharing parental responsibility and leaving the child in the home, removing the child from the home or seeking an adoption order. Unless the child stays at home or is adopted, the care order will remain in place until the child is 18, and local authorities have a duty to promote their welfare until the age of 21.

How can parents contest it?

The short answer is, with difficulty. There is provision for legal aid for parents or those with parental responsibility, but family members who wish to become party to the proceedings may be means-tested or unable to obtain legal aid. Additionally, for law firms to make any money from legal aid work, they must rely on the swift turn over of cases and it is questionable whether many of these solicitors can literally afford the time and care that is needed to pursue cases adequately on behalf of families.

As we have seen, most families who find themselves involved in care proceedings are on low incomes, often poorly educated yet faced with the full might of our very adversarial and middle-class legal system. In general, cases are not decided quickly, as the court will want to ensure that it has all the evidence and reports it needs before making a final decision.

There is therefore an initial hearing at which the court decides how the case will be prepared. This will involve deciding -

(a) Where the child will live until the final hearing
(b) Who they will see
(c) What reports and paperwork should be sent to court
(d) Timetabling, which usually means that the case should be completed within 26 weeks.

At this juncture parent/s must have secured a solicitor and must become involved in the court proceedings, as otherwise -

'decisions may be made about your child without you knowing'.[228]

The difficulty here is that by this point, parent/s may feel so angry and alienated that they do not proceed rationally. In my experience, they are often seething about the way in which they have been treated, or the inaccurate statements made about them, and are sick to the back teeth of being put into meetings in which no-one is there from family or friends to speak for them. If they were there, of course, the whole show might collapse into a shouting match, but this is where the sheer might and weight of the state prevails. It, and its agents, the social workers, local authority solicitors and medical 'experts' (who frequently make their living from doing the rounds of criminal and family courts and who are sometimes, finally discredited, as in the case of Sir Roy Meadows) are not at all emotionally involved in the case. They don't care about the family; they care only about the child, and even then only in so far as they have done their 'duty'. None of them will be looking for the child a decade later, amongst the homeless, the prison population and the paupers' graves. They will have forgotten

[228] www.frg.org.uk

child A, but the parents - however at fault they may be - will always remember their child; they are emotionally invested. Even the worst of them has more invested in that child than any employee. Despite this, and just because of the emotional volatility engendered when any mother - whether human, ursine or bovine - feels her young are being threatened, the parent/s may act irrationally, refuse to get involved, or to be proactive in their case.

For example, a parent who is thinking cogently and who understands the situation will know that they must have a fallback position ready to offer the court, should a care order be made. For example, they should immediately involve in the proceedings any family member who might make a suitable alternative carer, should a care order be made. They could then request that social workers assess them for suitability. That said, I have personally come across cases where grandparents have been distraught that they have been deemed unsuitable as carers because of disability, the 'contagion' of being close to the parent/s, lack of foster care funding making it impossible for them to manage, etc. Similarly, parent/s may find that contact is limited or non-existent. Under current law, it is the welfare of the child, not necessarily of their siblings, parents or wider family that is the principal consideration. Sadly, when children do return to care after a weekend at home, their emotional distress on returning to care is often blamed on the parents and seen as a reason to further curtail contact.

How can this be right?
It can largely be right for two reasons:
1. The public has been flooded with media cases of tragic child deaths (which in reality are rarely predicted)
2. Parents cannot go to the press about their case

Until relatively recently family proceedings were always held in private, with no friends or relatives allowed to attend unless they were directly involved in the case. Effectively parents had no witnesses to how their children were removed from their care and nothing said in court could be stated outside the courtroom. Parents were gagged and bound.

However following increasing pressure and more criticism of 'expert' advice which had lead to children wrongly being taken into care, new rules were introduced in 2010, allowing 'accredited' journalists to request permission to attend court. Obviously this means that journalists will want to be careful not to lose their accreditation, which may in turn consciously or subconsciously act as a brake. However, in reality the cases were not really of interest to journalists because they were so restricted in what they could report. They could, for example, only refer in general terms - allegations of violence - to the issues in hand, and not to the substance of the case on either side.

Although, in 2014, the President of the Family Division released a Guidance Note, requesting greater transparency be given to the work of the court, and that there be greater use in law reports of judgments made, these issues are left to the judge's discretion, and judges are divided on the matter. What is clear, however, is that unlike criminal cases, where supporters of the defendant may sit in the court, and where with little restriction, journalists are free to report, the Family Court remains firmly under the control of the judiciary and the state.

Whilst much of the secrecy can be said to be in place to protect the interests of the child or family, in reality it must inhibit the right to a fair 'trial'. Although parents may talk about their case to those who are involved in it, they may not talk about it to other people, or seek help from the wider public. Her Majesty's Courts Service states:

'You ... cannot share information about your proceedings to the public at large, or to a section of the public'.[229]

Whilst this same embargo applies to criminal cases, it is because the court does not want a jury to be influenced one way or another by unsafe evidence or gossip. However, there is no jury in the family court; the parents are quite alone. Arguably, this approach is in itself abusive, in threatening parents with consequences in order to stop them talking. It is not clear, however, why such secrecy is needed. Obviously names should not be used, or identifying features. But surely young children are unlikely to be affected if the parents wish to go public and older children could, and probably should, be consulted. Unfortunately, as we have seen, parents have little recourse to outside, independent, bodies. There is no Criminal Cases Review Commission (CCRC) to investigate alleged miscarriages of justice (after the appeal stage has failed) because 'trying' parents in the civil court and removing their children is not part of the criminal law.[230] Nor can parents at any point in care proceedings appeal to the independent Ombudsman, because the Local Government Ombudsman –

---

[229] HMCS (2016) *Can I talk about my case outside court? A guide for family court users. EX710.* http://www.childrenneedfamilies.co.uk/court-forms/EX710_web_0409.pdf

[230] The Criminal Cases Review Commission is the only body in its area of jurisdiction with the power to send a case back to an appeals court if it concludes that there is a real possibility that the court will overturn a conviction or reduce a sentence. Since starting work in 1997, it has on average referred 33 cases a year for appeal.

'can't look into complaints about anything that has been considered by a court. And we can't stop a council from taking court action that will affect you, for example if the council starts proceedings to take a child into care, or to have a child adopted.'[231]

One solution to the whole approach might to allow care proceedings only after the case has been heard in the criminal court. If a parent has abused or neglected a child, they have surely committed a crime that requires a trial and jury; a fair trial in other words. Upon a finding of guilt, a fine, a sentence of some sort (community where possible) and possibly care proceedings might then be appropriate.

We might also consider ending our adversarial, investigative style of child protection and adopting instead practices more akin to those in other European countries. For example, the French system is non-adversarial and channels child protection concerns through the 'juge des enfants', who has wide powers and who sets the agenda for social workers. In other European countries, the system of first pursuing a criminal conviction is already prevalent.[232]

Adoption

We know that historically, and still today, voluntary adoption - where the parent/s choose to give up their child to adoption - is often motivated by social considerations. Just as, in the first half of the 20th

[231] Local Government Ombudsman, *Children's care services*. http://www.lgo.org.uk/make-a-complaint/fact-sheets/social-care/children-s-care-services, accessed 1/3/2017

[232] Hill M (Ed) (1991) *Social work in the European community: the social policy and practice contexts*. Jessica Kingsley

century, the stigma of being an unmarried mother, at a time when abortion was illegal, was a driver to give up a baby for adoption, so today, too, parents still sometimes feel forced, for one reason or another, to give up a child for adoption. What is more unusual about England and Wales is that we have a system whereby at any point from birth onwards, a child may be taken from a parent and placed for adoption, with the parent/s losing all rights to the child. It goes without saying that almost all the 'bad' parents are poor. It is estimated that 90% of forced adoptions are of children living below the poverty line.[233]

This practice, commonly called 'forced adoption', means that just as with an application for a care order, local authorities can seek a 'freeing' and adoption order from the Family Court with parent/s again forced to defend themselves. This of course is invariably much harder to do, when - for example - a single mother has her child taken from her whilst still on the maternity ward. This is fairly common practice, and of course is not only devastating to the mother but also comes at a time when she is in no position to respond to proceedings, attend meetings or defend herself in court. Further, section 14 of the Children and Families Act 2014, which sets a statutory time limit of 26 weeks for the conclusion of care proceedings unless there are 'exceptional' reasons, adds to the pressure. It will be said that the welfare of the child is paramount and that therefore a speedy conclusion and permanent settlement is appropriate. However, it should also be noted that, again, if parents later manage to 'prove' that an error was made, there is no way that the child can be returned to them. Interestingly, the Council of Europe has criticised this interpretation of the welfare of

[233] https://en.m.wikipedia.org/wiki/Forced_adoption_in_the_United_Kingdom. Accessed 5/3/2017

the child, yet still the process continues. In its summary, the Council of Europe report notes:

> 'Member states should themselves put into place laws, regulations and procedures which truly put the best interest of the child first in removal, placement and reunification decisions. The competent European Council body should develop policy guidelines for member states on how to avoid practices deemed abusive in this context, namely (except in exceptional circumstances) severing family ties completely, removing children from parental care at birth; basing placement decisions on the effluxion of time and having recourse to adoption without parental consent'.[234]

By 'effluxion', the Council of Europe means the passing of time, in the sense that judges in England and Wales may rule that as the baby has now spent six months with foster carers who wish to adopt him, he is now settled and therefore, given 'the welfare of the child' principle, time in itself is a reason for denying the birth parents their natural rights. In paragraphs 72-74, the report makes clear that England and Wales are the culprits:

> 'England and Wales are really unique in Europe in placing so many children for adoption, in particular in the young age groups which is

---

[234] Council of Europe (15 March 2015) *Social services in Europe: Legislation and practice and the removal of children from their families in EC member states.* Doc 13730. http://semantic-pace.net/tools/pdf.aspx?doc=aHR0cDovL2Fzc2VtYmx5LmNvZS5pbnQvbncveG1sL1hSZWYvWDJILURXLWV4dHIuYXNwP2ZpbGVpZD0yMTU2NyZsYW5nPUVO&xsl=aHR0cDovL3NlbWFudGljGljcGFjZS5uZXQvWHNsdC9QZGYvWFJlZi1XRC1BVC1YTUwyUERGLnhzbA==&xsltparams=ZmlsZWlkPTIxNTY3 . Accessed 5/3/2017

"popular" on the adoption market. . . . The former Prime Minister Tony Blair went so far as to establish 'adoption targets' for local authorities'.

Crucially, the report goes on to identify our misunderstanding of the welfare of the child and to emphasise that parents should almost always have contact with their children. Paragraph 12 states:

"The European Court of Human Rights, based on the European Convention on Human Rights (ETS No. 5), has summarised the legal situation well in the case of Neulinger and Shuruk v. Switzerland (judgment of 6 July 2010) . . .
'In this area the decisive issue is whether a fair balance between the competing interests at stake – those of the child, of the two parents, and of public order – has been struck, within the margin of appreciation afforded to States in such matters ..., bearing in mind, however, that the child's best interests must be the primary consideration .... The child's best interests may, depending on their nature and seriousness, override those of the parents .... The parents' interests, especially in having regular contact with their child, nevertheless remain a factor when balancing the various interests at stake".'

In other words, the welfare of the child in the majority of cases dictates that there should be contact with birth parents, because the child's welfare is not something that can be judged in one moment of time - the date of the court hearing, for example - but is something that stretches forward in time until the end of their lives. Consequently, whatever the short-term position, in almost every case children should retain contact with their parents, and adoption avoided.

Further, the same Council of Europe report reiterates a point made elsewhere in this book, that while there is evidence that the parents of children taken into care or forcibly adopted are predominantly on low incomes/below the poverty line and socially marginalised, there is no evidence that these social groups parent worse than more affluent parents. There is only evidence that they are more likely to seek help from public funds/agencies (because they cannot afford other support or help) and that they are far far more likely to have their children taken into care. Such was the report's concern on this point, that it states:

'Statistical analyses providing an authentic vision of which groups of children are more exposed to being removed from their families is also lacking, though evidence suggests that children from vulnerable groups are disproportionately represented in the care population of member States. There is, however, no evidence to suggest that, in similar contexts, parents who are poor, less educated, belong to an ethnic or religious minority or have a migration background are more likely to abuse or neglect their children. . .

Financial and material poverty should never be the only justification for the removal of a child from parental care, but should be seen as a signal for the need to provide appropriate support to the family. Moreover, it is not enough to show that a child could be placed in a more beneficial environment for its upbringing to remove a child from his or her parents and even less to sever family ties completely.'[235]

---

[235] Council of Europe (15 March 2015) *op.cit.* p.3, paras 4&5.

Interestingly, France 5 produced a documentary, which translates as 'England's Stolen Children' and which was aired on French television in November 2016. The French view of our system was summed up as follows:

'"*This documentary tells the story of the thousands of children unjustly removed from their families. It chronicles families' terrifying experiences of children taken at birth, the promise of future removal whilst mothers are pregnant and the threat of removal directed at women who have not yet had children, solely on a suspicion of future harm to the child. The setting for this documentary is not a lawless, tyrannical country where child rights do not exist – these tragedies are unfolding in a State which is bound by European legislation and is one of France's neighbours: The United Kingdom. The film reveals an unthinkable practice: every year, Great Britain sets quotas for the number of children it must remove from parents in order to facilitate adoptions. If these quotas are not met, the local authorities have to pay financial penalties and their budget is revised and ultimately decreased.*

Private sector companies, sometimes listed on the stock exchange, are often tasked with placing children with adoptive parents. Children are "advertised" by these agencies, their details completely exposed and publicly available, with descriptions which include 'sellable' qualities such as positive personality traits. . .
Maltreatment in the context of Great Britain's Forced Adoption practices does not need to be evidenced. A suspicion of future maltreatment raised by social services is all that's needed for a child to be taken away from their parents forever. In Great Britain, child

protection has become skewed by a broadbrush perspective which presumes that struggling families and single mothers can never provide stable homes or make good parents.

This Human Rights scandal in the heart of Europe stays hidden inside Britain's borders. The law prevents parents and journalists from telling these stories, with the threat of jail if they break their silence. They don't even have the right to mention the name of the child that's been stolen."[236]

One of the problems with legislation and policy in England and Wales is that it appears rational. Despite the continual findings of abuse in care, the ruined lives, the homeless and prison populations so full of care leavers, it is all blamed on the parents. At the time of writing, the British Government set up, in March 2015, the Independent Inquiry into Child Sexual Abuse, which has been dogged by resignations and turmoil. Now under the chairmanship of Alexis Jay, who exposed the massive scale of sexual abuse (much of it of children on care orders or in care) in Rotherham, it has begun to take evidence. One of the first bodies to give evidence has been the Child Migrants Trust.[237]

More than 130,000 children were removed or encouraged away from their families and sent to an ostensibly wonderful life in Canada, New Zealand, Zimbabwe (formerly Rhodesia) and Australia. The reality for many was quite different: beatings, isolation, and sexual abuse, and they are now at last, sadly, being heard. Too late for many of them,

---

[236] http://m.france5.fr/emissions/le-monde-en-face/les-enfants-voles-d-angleterre_520481 Researching Reform https://researchingreform.net/2016/11/14/englands-stolen-children-controversial-new-documentary-on-forced-adoption/ accessed 14/3/2017

[237] www.childmigrantstrust.com

who could never trace their families, too late for the mothers and fathers who never saw their children again. For the charities involved, it was part of their raison d'etre. Their business model was and is care and even today they use the photographs of sad looking children to generate revenue from the public. They have never been given the criticism they deserve. Yet each time a scandal breaks, whether it is forced migration, Rotherham, Pindown, Frank Beck, Oxford, North Wales, Rochdale, Plymouth, or any of the myriad of places, it is dismissed as an anomaly. It's time to change, to rethink the structure of British law and policy, and to really care about our children and families.

KEY FINDINGS

1) The Children Act 1989, as amended and subsequent Acts are continuations of a Poor Law model that punishes rather than redeems the poor, using the carrot and stick model.

2) Our legislations is at odds with what many would consider a fair and proper reading of Article 3 of the UN Convention on the Rights of the Child, and Articles 6 and 8 of the Human Rights Act 1998.

3) Making the welfare of the child **the** paramount consideration rather than **a** primary consideration has led to a distorted view of the welfare of the child over time, and the welfare of its siblings and family.

4) Changing the Children Act 1989 and subsequent legislation to ensure that the needs of the child and family are a primary consideration, and changing to a more holistic model that builds on

strengths as evidenced in other European countries may provide a way forward.

5) The question of whether a child 'is suffering or is likely to suffer significant harm' does not include any reference to outcomes from care, or the harm caused by such loss to siblings or parents.

6) We have an inquisitorial and adversarial system in which parents may lose their children for life without their case being made public, and without the right to be heard and judged by a jury.

7) Options for change include making criminal convictions a prerequisite before care proceedings can be taken, or greater use of non-adversarial routes such as are used in France and several other European countries.

8) The Government propose to make it illegal to sell a puppy below the age of 8 weeks.[238] Babies however may be forcibly adopted at birth from parents who are considered unsuitable - a practice frowned upon by many Europeans and seen as contrary to the human rights of all involved.

QUESTIONS FOR DISCUSSION

a) How might our core children and families legislation be improved to reflect a public health model of family well-being?

b) If the law does not set out exactly what causes 'significant harm' and what would constitute evidence for it, how can it have universal meaning?

c) It is right to effectively try parents in civil courts that require no juries?

---

[238]https://www.gov.uk/government/news/new-plans-to-crack-down-on-backstreet-puppy-breeders

d) How might parental involvement in initial inquiries and strategy meetings be enabled in law, and how might the system be rendered less adversarial?

e) Can it be right to ask young children what they want, when they are too young to understand the implications of what they say, even though they understand the questions?

CHAPTER SIX

THE CHILD AND FAMILY SOCIAL WORKER -
A REAL PROFESSION

Conclusions

This book has sought to argue that for the vast majority of looked after children, care is not the answer. In a world in which evidence bases for actions are routinely demanded, research cannot demonstrate that care has either 'saved' a child's life or improved it. It is demonstrably arguable that a prolonged period in care (of more than a few weeks) may lead to inexorable psychological damage. We have to accept that, at the tipping point, we cannot prevent random or inexplicable acts of violence against children, but we certainly can try to prevent that tipping point from being reached. We know who is likely to harm a child, we know that we could prevent it. We have to accept that we will never prevent all deaths at parents' hands, nor will we ever eradicate poor or inadequate parenting, but we can make huge inroads into doing so.

Chapter four on public health solutions indicated ways in which critical outcomes can be prevented. We know from the many books and research papers on this subject, how parenting can be improved. We also know that some parents are 'hard to reach'. Yet this reticence to connect with services offered by in various forms by the state or social workers, is clearly understandable; they are often seen almost as the 'enemy'. We also know that in general, parents are not subject to investigation. However, those who are known to social services either as an adult or a child are far more likely to come under scrutiny as are those who have to ask for help. The middle and upper classes do not need to ask for help because they have the money to purchase help, and they know that asking can be a double-edged sword. For some, who have had positive experiences of social work, support is welcomed; but for others, disengagement is the only solution. Similarly, as we have seen in earlier chapters, many cases of child homicide were perpetrated by parents who had been (sometimes surprisingly) invisible to the authorities such as violent men or psychiatrically disturbed mothers. In both cases, despair may often turn to anger and a feeling that 'taking the children with me' is the only solution. Helping these parents to articulate their feelings without threat of proceedings, and to obtain the support they need is vital.

Social workers who deal with depressed or suicidal people are urged to 'ask the suicide question', in order to explore not only how likely it is (by ideation of method, for example) that the person will complete, but also to open up that whole discussion as to what might help. No-one is taught to ask the 'I'll kill them' question. Even if they asked it, they might be unlikely to receive an honest answer, because however desperate the parent, they are reluctant to hand over their children to the unknown. We understand this in the animal kingdom. We know not to step between a mother bear and its cubs, or a cow and its calf, yet for some reason we blame parents who are threatened by the state. By radically reducing 'care' and opening up training and support, we may yet enable that parent to admit their darkest thoughts in the knowledge that they will get the help and support they need. That in turn requires a properly trained work force.

Rethinking Social Work Training

Many believe that current social work training in the UK falls well below the standard needed for the rigours of assessing and providing help to children and their parents. Following the death of Baby P and the second Laming report, the Labour government published the findings of the Social Work Taskforce and set up the Social Work Reform Board and the College of Social Work. The College of Social Work has now disappeared, and to an outsider, the provision of social work training has barely altered. There are two new entry routes into the 'profession': Frontline and Step Up, with a remit to specifically focus on the knowledge and skills to work effectively with children and families. However, the main route into social work remains the social work degree, a three year course, or a two year Masters degree.

Despite the inquiries and reports, the teaching offered by most universities has not radically changed since 2009; this despite an excellent report by Sir Martin Narey (2014)[239] calling for a radical overhaul of child and family academic training, which had been commissioned by the then Minister Michael Gove. To a great extent, the courses teach the same modules as they have taught for years. For example, Bath University offered, for 2018, the following modules:

YEAR 1

Community needs assessment, groups and teamwork in practice
Social problems and social policy
Introduction to social work
Understanding society: Britain in global context
Social work and life course 1
Social policy, welfare and the state
Classical sociological theory
Social work and life course 2
Readiness for direct social work practice

---

[239] Department for Education (2014) *Making the education of social workers consistently effective: report of Sir Martin Narey's independent review of the education of children's social workers.* London:TSOhttps://www.gov.uk/government/uploads/system/uploads/attachment_data/file/287756/Making_the_education_of_social_workers_consistently_effective.pdf

YEAR 2

Critical reflection on professional practice 1
Discrimination and empowerment: skills in practice
Social work practice placement year 2
Theories and methods in social work
Social work with children and families 1
Mental health social work 1
Social work with adults 1

YEAR 3

Social work with children and families 2
Working in a social care organisation
Mental health social work 2
Social work with adults 2
Critical reflection on professional practice 2
Social work practice case study
Social work practice placement year 3

These topics are all that are needed to call yourself a child and family social worker. There is no requirement to understand the benefits system, debt management, how to talk to parents and children, research methods (in order to understand whether what you are reading has any reference in fact), complex aspects of child development or parenting etc.

But Bath is not alone; the vast majority of universities offering the social work degree offer the same sort of modules. Nor is teaching proportionate to need. Bath University sets out the contact time, as follows:[240]

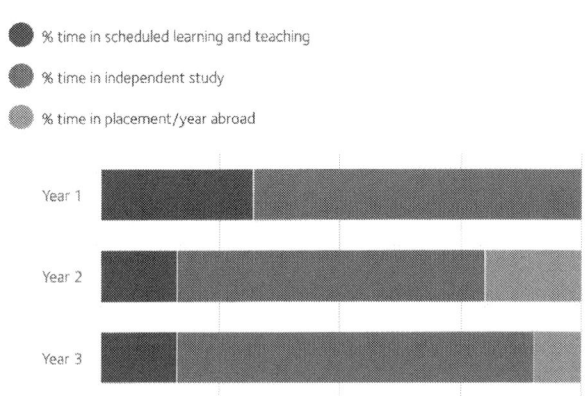

In other words there is barely a year's worth of teaching in a three year period, let alone any tutorials or seminars. My focus here on Bath University is random; that website just happened to come first on an internet search. Readers may search for themselves. An inspection of The Complete University Guide for 2018, shows Bath as coming 4th in the UK-wide league table for social work. First is Nottingham.[241] Below is their current curriculum for a social work degree that will qualify young people to work with our most vulnerable children and families:

---

[240] http://www.bath.ac.uk/courses/undergraduate-2018/social-work/bsc-social-work-and-applied-social-studies/?gclid=EAlalQobChMlxt7E29rq1glVQuEbCh2VOgznEAAYASAAEgli0fD_BwE

[241] https://www.thecompleteuniversityguide.co.uk/league-tables/rankings?s=social%20work

'Typical year one modules

Core modules

Communication Skills for Practice

Introduction to Social Work

Investigating Social Worlds

Policy and Social Justice

Understanding Contemporary Society

Typical year two modules

Core modules

From Theory to Practice

Human Growth and Development Across the Life Course

Law for Social Work

Political Theory and Social Policy

Social Work Research

Plus:Practice Learning 1 - 80-day placement

Typical year three modules

Core modules

Critical Perspectives on Social Work

Safeguarding

Either:

Social Work with Adults

 or

Social Work with Children and Families

Plus: Practice Learning 2 - 90-day placement'[242]

---

[242] http://www.nottingham.ac.uk/ugstudy/courses/sociologyandsocialpolicy/social-work.aspx
accessed 12/10/2017

Perhaps even more worryingly, Nottingham University adds, as a footnote -

'The modules we offer are inspired by the research interests of our staff and as a result may change for reasons of, for example, research developments or legislation changes. The above list is a sample of typical modules we offer, not a definitive list.'

In other words, the content of a taught social work degree, which qualifies someone to be a social worker in the UK, depends not on the needs of children and families (or any other group) but on the research interests of staff.

There is no point in going through all the universities, because in a sense the point is, I believe, made. Whilst the Munro report and second Laming report,[243] for example, tended to focus on the context in which social work is practised and the structural deficits in local authority departments, the reality is that despite lip service being paid to changes in social work training, little has happened. Narey, for example, also stressed the importance of improving the calibre of social work student, yet even at Nottingham, the entry requirements reflect the fact that whilst ABB at A level might be desirable, they will be flexible. My own experience from a decade spent teaching social work is that 'bums on seats' for Hefce funding[244] and an empathy with less academic but nevertheless kind and helpful people, are more important than sticking to admission tariffs.

---

[243] Department of Education (2011) *The Monro review of child protection: final report - a child centred system.* Cmnd 8062. https://www.gov.uk/government/uploads/system/uploads/attachment_data/file/175391/Munro-Review.pdf
The Lord Laming (2009) *The protection of children in England: a progress report.* HC330. London. https://www.gov.uk/government/uploads/system/uploads/attachment_data/file/328117/The_Protection_of_Children_in_England.pdf

[244] Higher Education Funding Council for England

There is a place for everyone in social work, but not necessarily a place for everyone to be a qualified social worker. Much of what we all do every day is social work: helping people, volunteering, enabling and so on, but a professional social worker needs to be more than this. They need to be academically strong in order to understand the complex needs not only of parents and children but of Courts, the law and the NHS. Those who write reports for child protection case conferences, CAFCASS (the Child and Family Court Advisory and Support Service), the Family Court, adoption/fostering or for head teachers need to be able to approach the task with a fully prepared tool box that leaves no stone unturned in pursuing the wellbeing of families, and need to be able to not only articulate clearly and non-defensively their analysis of any given situation, but also to write it up and present it in a fashion that is succinct, accurate and well researched. But even if the admissions bar were to be set at a higher level, much more needs to be done at an academic level to make a social worker in children and families a credible professional.

It is surely time to offer social work training that is perhaps more akin to that of medicine. In the UK, doctors, for example, train for five or six years before beginning full-time on the wards as junior doctors. There is a clear pathway post qualifying, with exams (not easily downloadable essays or coursework) to demarcate each progression until consultant status is reached. In general, the population has confidence in its doctors and consultants; the same cannot be said for social workers. Of course there are excellent social workers out there now, but it is the result more of chance than of appropriate professional training.

There is, then, surely a case for developing separate social work training strands, with a new social work degree in child and family support being developed. Such a degree would demand a high calibre of student, a four year course and content devoted to child and family support. A suggested curriculum - but there is room for debate - might be:

Year 1- Understanding Context
Social policy
Understanding the benefit system
Child and family legal framework
An introduction to research methods/understanding what makes 'good' research
Simple child development (1)
Parent mental health (1)
Listening and talking to families (1)
Placement (8 weeks)

Year 2
What is good parenting?
Complex child development (2)
Disabled parenting
Childhood disabilities and support
Parent mental health (2)
Substance misuse and parenting
Active listening to children and families (2)
Placement (8 weeks)

Year 3
Domestic violence facts/policy/law
Children with emotional and behavioural difficulties - support and dilemmas
Youth offending - causes and solutions
Legal framework/benefits and family support in action

The nuts and bolts of child protection

3 month placement within statutory local authority child and family setting.

Year 4

Supporting parent/s and children through domestic violence

How does child protection work?

Law and casework on child protection

Working with psychiatrically ill parents.

Working with dual diagnosis parents to enable family support

Working with families to enable children in care to be reunited

3 month placement in statutory local authority setting

At least 50% of modules to be examinable with remainder of modules involving at least three witten essays each, with degree awarded on completion of -

(a) Exams/coursework to satisfactory standard at each year end.

(b) Placement portfolio

(c) Dissertation

As happens now, newly qualified social workers might then take up supervised employment as child and family social workers for a probationary two year period. Continuing professional development thereafter might consist of a requirement to be up-to-date with the benefit system and the law as it affects children and families, with set exams in further specialisms until the equivalent of Consultant Child and Family Social worker is reached.

Changing social work training and challenging current thinking on child protection is only a small part of a much wider jigsaw. The attrition rate for social workers is high, and many local authorities struggle to find and keep staff. A properly trained and professional body might be adequately rewarded financially and possibly more permanent with clearer career pathways. But a large part of the problem, as others such as Lord Laming and Munro have pointed out, is to be found in the structural inertia of local authorities. This book cannot cover that ground, which is critical and important. It seeks only to encourage readers and policy makers to rethink child protection and to rethink our profession. That cannot be achieved whilst those who work at the coal face day in and day out have little professional standing. Whether working in the statutory/local authority/charity or private sector, child and family social workers need to take ownership of their 'profession', to challenge procedures/Guidance and law where necessary and to ensure that their voice is heard. Too often they have spoken out, only to find themselves sidelined. It is not good enough that inquiries and task forces should be led by retired judges and academics when the people who do the job actually know how it is; they just do not have the kudos to be heard. But more than this, unless child and family social workers are well trained and rigorously examined, they cannot inspire trust amongst those they seek to serve, and nor will they have the skills and knowledge necessary to help them.

This book seeks to place families first, to provide a more effectual and pragmatic approach to ensuring that all our children are safe and cared for. Working alongside them to achieve that, we need rigorously trained and professional Child and Family Social Workers who can command respect at the highest government and intra-governmental level. It is what our families deserve.

KEY FINDINGS

1) A public health approach to enabling parents and reducing numbers in care requires a properly trained and recognisably professional work force.

2) Current social work training in children and families is woefully inadequate.

3) There should be a separate Child and Family Social Work degree that has a singular focus, is longer, far more rigorous, demands a far higher course entry tariff and which properly prepares students for a profession.

4) Career progression to be structured, rigorous and examinable until Consultant level is reached.

Questions for Discussion

a) What form should any new degree in Child and Family Social Work take?

b) To what extent should there be a requirement that the degree includes tutorials and seminars, as well as exams.

c) Given that many student placements fall short of the experience needed, how can the placements offered be better provided and monitored?

The End

This book was self published, as mainstream publishers and reviewers tend not to want to challenge current paradigms. However you feel about this book, I hope that it has been of some help to you. It would be great if you could leave a review - good or bad - on the Amazon website at:
https://www.amazon.co.uk/RADICAL-CHILD-PROTECTION-APPROACH-Reducing/dp/1976713447

I have also created a website with research articles which you may find useful:
www.socialworkwithchildrenandfamilies.org

Many thanks for reading this far, and wishing you well, Charlotte Ritchie

Printed in Great Britain
by Amazon

41282116R10118